A HOUSE OF MANY BLESSINGS

A House of Many Blessings

Quin Sherrer
and
Laura Watson

VINE
BOOKS

Servant Publications
Ann Arbor, Michigan

Vine Books is an imprint of Servant Publications especially designed
to serve Evangelical Christians.

The "NIV" and "New International Version" trademarks are
registered in the United States Patent and Trademark Office by
International Bible Society.

Other versions quoted are abbreviated as follows: AMP, *The
Amplified Bible*, Old Testament copyright © 1965, 1987 by the
Zondervan Corporation and the Amplified New Testament
copyright © 1958, 1987 by the Lockman Foundation, used by
permission; NKJV, *New King James Version*, copyright © 1979,
1980, 1982 by Thomas Nelson Inc., Publishers, used by permission;
TLB, *The Living Bible*, © 1971 by Tyndale House Publishers, used
by permission; NASB, *New American Standard Bible*, copyright ©
1960, 1962, 1963, 1968, 1971, 1972, 1973, 1975, 1977 by the
Lockman Foundation, used by permission; KJV, *King James
Version*, the Authorized Version, Zondervan Publishing House,
used by permission.

Published by Servant Publications
P.O. Box 8617
Ann Arbor, MI 48107

Cover design by Graphicus Corporation

93 94 95 96 97 10 9 8 7 6 5 4 3 2 1

Printed in the United States of America

ISBN 0-89283-815-9

Library of Congress Cataloging-in-Publication Data

Sherrer, Quin.
    A house of many blessings / Quin Sherrer and Laura Watson.
        p.   cm
    ISBN 0-89283-815-9
    1. Hospitality--Religious aspects--Christianity.   I. Watson, Laura.
    II. Title.
    BV4647.H67S55   1993
    241'.671—dc20   93-3053

In memory of
Jamie Buckingham
our friend, mentor, pastor.

He taught us
how to pray,
how to write, and
how to be hospitable.

In Appreciation

Our appreciation to Pastor Peter Lord of Park Avenue Baptist Church, Titusville, Florida, who gave us written permission to quote freely from two booklets Quin Sherrer wrote for his church in the late 1970s: "Let's Practice Hospitality" and "Decorating Our Homes to Please the Lord" (Agape Ministries, Titusville, Florida).

...to Strang Communications for permission to use excerpts from articles Quin has written for *Charisma* magazine.

...to the Tabernacle Church, Melbourne, Florida, for permission to use excerpts from articles Laura has written for their publication, *The Trumpet*.

Contents

Foreword

DURING MY THIRTY-EIGHT YEARS of marriage to Jamie Bucking-ham, our home was always open to others. Jamie—the generous, loving man that he was—was forever inviting someone to come visit us, whether it was another minister and his family, a missionary back in the States on furlough, or a young single mother and her children with no place else to go. Jamie believed in following the direction of Paul in Romans 12:13: "Share with God's people who are in need. Practice hospitality."

I will be honest with you. Sometimes being hospitable was not easy. Sometimes it was downright inconvenient. I remember getting weary once and complaining to God, Jamie, and anyone else within earshot that I was tired of having so much company. Then the Lord led me to read Matthew 10:41a: "Anyone who receives a prophet because he is a prophet will receive a prophet's reward."

Talk about motivation! Over the years Jamie and I received many servants of God into our home. Boldly, I began to claim every reward laid up for them for myself, too!

It was not always easy to prepare big meals, change bed-sheets, wash extra loads of towels, and otherwise have my normal routine turned upside down at the ring of a doorbell. But the act of inviting outsiders in, of being hospitable, reaped joys and rewards I would never have known if I hadn't opened that door.

I learned early on—fortunately, for it probably saved my sanity—that my family did not necessarily have to do a whole lot when company came in. With Jamie's help, I learned that all we had to do was be ourselves—and our visitors would take us as we were. When someone came in, we would say, "Make yourself at home. Become part of the family while you are here." That always made our guests feel comfortable. And it took a load of responsibility off of me.

My five children—now grown, with children of their own—were real troopers. They had more opportunities than most kids to learn the lessons—and the joys—of giving and sharing. I could not begin to count the number of times Jamie and I asked them to give up their bedrooms and bunk in with one another in order to make room for "a few extra."

But each of them learned to love our visitors as much as Jamie and I did—especially the missionaries. They would sit in wonder and awe as they listened to the most amazing real-life bedtime stories—tales of planes filled with Bibles flying over the jungle, of faraway tribesmen laying down their weapons to hear more about Jesus, and of "God's smugglers" courageously crossing over Communist borders to share the Good News. The richness of those contacts has had a profound impact on their lives, and their own efforts to be hospitable today are now having an impact on a third generation of Buckinghams.

I believe hospitality is not only a gift but a mandate which we, as Christians, should practice. "Love one another," the Bible says. John makes plain that when we love one another, we are showing our love for God. When we are serving others, we are serving God.

My good friends, Quin and Laura, with a sensitivity led by the Holy Spirit, have included in this volume all the facets involved in Christ-centered hospitality. In addition to gaining an understanding of the spiritual implications and rewards of being hospitable, you will find a lot of good, practical advice on how to make your house a home—one that is open to serving God's people, whether they are relatives, friends, or strangers. I encourage you to take their suggestions to heart. After all, who knows when you may have an opportunity to entertain "angels unawares" (Heb 13:2 KJV).

Jackie Buckingham
Palm Bay, Florida

Introduction

And they were continually devoting themselves to the apostles'
teaching and to fellowship, to the breaking of bread and to
prayer.... And day by day continuing with one mind in the
temple, and breaking bread from house to house, they were tak-
ing their meals together with gladness and sincerity of heart,
praising God, and having favor with all the people.

Acts 2:42, 46, 47a NASB

HOSPITALITY: Reaching out to those God puts in your path.
Hospitality must be very important to God—it is one of the
qualifications listed for elders in 1 Timothy 3:2.

What does Jesus say that makes us think we need to practice
hospitality? It was at mealtime that Jesus revealed himself. When
he broke the bread at the Last Supper with his disciples in the
upper room, he said, "This is my body, which is for you..." (1
Cor 11:24b). He told us to recognize the body of Christ when
we remember him by taking communion.

Jamie Buckingham, in serving communion, would remind us
that we are to see Jesus in one another—*we* are his body. Put
that way, he makes our efforts at hospitality easy.

We are encouraged by other Scriptures, including 1 Peter
4:9-10:

Offer hospitality to one another without grumbling. Each
one should use whatever gift he has received to serve others,
faithfully administering God's grace in its various forms.

One of the most outspoken prophets of our time, David
Wilkerson, has warned, "There is coming an acceleration of

events more amazing and frightful than all changes of previous years."

As added pressures, adjustments, and fiery trials loom ahead—and are now upon us—Christians must become more sensitive to ways their homes can be used to extend fellowship. Those who have never looked at their homes as *tools of ministry* will be challenged to do so. How? By biblical examples.

Right after the outpouring of the Holy Spirit on the Day of Pentecost, believers began meeting to devote themselves to four things:

- to the apostles' teaching
- to fellowship
- to breaking of bread
- to prayer

Notice that they not only went to the temple, but their homes became "small sanctuaries" or temples for teaching, prayer, fellowship, and meals.

OUR GOAL

From a background of not having much to spend for food or decorating, I (Quin) learned not only to make-do but to make-beautiful. The secret was letting the older women in the church teach me. That is what Laura and I—both "older women"— want to do here. Laura's background was different from mine, but still influenced by a family affected by the Great Depression. We are writing together, but we will use me (Quin) to tell the story to keep the book from being unwieldy.

Laura and I have been a praying and writing team for many years. It was Jamie Buckingham—to whose memory this book is lovingly dedicated—who introduced us and suggested our rooming together at an upcoming writers' workshop. There we discovered that I (a journalist) am the idea and story-gathering person, and Laura is the one with the ability to put it all together.

In this book we will give you creative ways our homes can be used as an avenue for fellowship, prayer, teaching, and breaking of bread. We will share with you how to serve one another, pray for one another, teach one another, have the same care for one another, receive one another, and show hospitality to one another.

As a sanctuary for family and those God sends our way, our homes can be a safe place to experience Jesus' love extended through our hands.

To practice hospitality we have to do it over and over. Opening our homes may seem foreign to some who need to break free from a bondage of intimidation. We recognize others cannot use their homes, perhaps due to a spouse's objections. But they, too, can be hospitable in other ways.

While hospitality often falls on the shoulders of wives, it is not limited to married women. All Christians are encouraged to offer hospitality: husbands, wives, parents, children, single men and single women. Our book will focus more on a married woman's perspective but the creative ways we suggest to show hospitality can be adapted for almost any situation: living alone or living with others, large or small families, rich in material possessions or living on a limited income.

When we realize a Christian's material possessions are gifts from God, given to be used for God's purposes, we are off on an exciting adventure. We will allow the Lord to use us, our homes, and our possessions in creative ways we might never have considered before.

Ask our Lord to make yours a house of many blessings.

Quin Sherrer
P. O. Box 25433
Colorado Springs, CO
80936-5433

Laura Watson
1697 Willard Road NW
Palm Bay, FL 32907

PART ONE

Blessings of a Home

1

Welcome
to Our Home

(The Lord) blesses the home of the righteous.

Proverbs 3:33b

S IXTY-EIGHT, SIXTY-NINE, SEVENTY... "How many more steps do I have to climb, Sherry?" I asked, puffing. My youngest daughter and her Danish husband, Kim Christian, were taking me to their apartment in Copenhagen where they had lived for a year.

"Mom, there are only seventy-five steps. We live on the top floor, remember," she said nonchalantly.

Her letters had tried to prepare me for their living quarters. No elevator. No bathtub or built-in shower. A two-burner out-dated stove. A tiny refrigerator which doesn't make ice. "It is very hard to find apartments, but you will like ours," she had written.

When we finally dragged all my luggage up all those steps, Kim unlocked the door and Sherry flung it open with a flourish: "Velkommen til vores hjem, Mor! Welcome to our home, Mother!"

By my standards it was uncommonly modest. But Sherry and Kim had painted the walls a light cream, covered the floors with rugs and over the long narrow windows hung peach curtains which Sherry had made out of sheets. They had bought only a few pieces of Danish furniture, and that was it. But the peach tablecloth and fresh flowers on their living room table added color and warmth.

In the bedroom a few wall plaques and pictures reflected serenity. Their room said to me: "This is our sanctuary. Here is where we come for rest and for spiritual renewal, to read our Bible, to pray, to love."

I marveled that my daughter, brought up in twentieth-century America, had adapted so well. Even though it takes eons for her old stove to bake, every week she makes homemade bread. How could Sherry adjust to walking up five flights of stairs just to bring in the groceries? Or down to dump the garbage? How could she maneuver a bicycle everywhere she wanted to go, with so many buses and cars clogging the busy downtown streets? How had she learned her husband's language so well, so quickly?

But she had accepted this as home, I realized as I sat on their starkly simple couch, sipping tea. Would I be so diligent? So satisfied? So uncomplaining? So willing to make do and fix up?

ACCEPT MY HOME

How I wish I had known at her age how to do that—accept my house, no matter what. For years I was embarrassed to tears to let anyone see where we lived. I thought back to the Christmas night when I helped LeRoy, my husband of one hour, pack up all our earthly belongings. Hospitality was the last thing on my mind, as we crammed our wedding presents and a few of LeRoy's Air Force duds along with my suitcases into the back of his old green car. We were striking out for engineering college, our honeymoon just a stopover on our way.

Something inside me shouted all the way to Houston, "Whoopee, only one man to feed!" I could not imagine what it would be like to sit across the table from just one man—for a lifetime. Almost heaven, I thought.

For ten years my mother had operated a boarding house in Tallahassee, Florida to help support and educate her four children; I was the oldest. Since she served family style, all you could eat for seventy-five cents, each day in her dining room she fed from three hundred to six hundred men—college boys, construction crews, and state legislature workers.

My, how they could eat! "Shove the potatoes down this way, man. Don't hog the rolls," one would shout to another seated at the far end of one of the long tables. I watched in unending amazement as they devoured bowls heaped high with corn on the cob, pole beans, black-eyed peas, new potatoes, and yellow squash. Or mounds of Southern fried chicken, baked ham, or succulent roast beef slices. Hot yeast rolls—my mother's special recipe—brought fresh from the ovens by the dozens, were smothered in butter and cane syrup. My sister and I were often the only girls eating in the dining room crowded with all those men.

Yes, I resolved, when I marry, cooking for one man will be a snap. I certainly did not want to be bothered with having a bunch of people at my dining table either.

It never occurred to me that this bride had not even learned to cook yet—although I had tried often enough. My mother's main kitchen helper, lovingly called Big Cook, would shoo me away from her stove whenever I peeped over her ample shoulder to watch how she made her pineapple delight. But she shouted, "Get on out of here now," and handed me a bowlful of the creamy pineapple custard. "You will have plenty of time to learn to cook when you marry. Besides, honey, you won't be cooking for three hundred men."

Five days after our wedding LeRoy and I moved into a tiny off-campus walk-up apartment in Houston with mismatched overstuffed furniture and limp curtains.

Some weeks later I shouted at LeRoy, "I hate this apartment! I dearly hate it," hurling a pillow against the wall near where he sat studying at an old, rusty fold-up aluminum table. When the pillow hit, a bit of the sea-green wallpaper flecked off and floated down to the bare floor.

"Hush, the landlady downstairs will hear you," he warned, leaning over to retrieve the pillow. "Shouting won't fix anything, anyway."

"I hope she does hear me. For what she is charging us, she could afford to fix up this place. I don't see how she can expect anyone to live in this dump."

Within six months I was already longing for my mother's old house back in Florida. But I was stuck. My only hope was that as soon as LeRoy got his engineering degree, we could leave. In the meantime, both of us had to work to pay for his tuition and rent on this horrid apartment. I was glad it was a temporary dwelling. Surely not my home.

WHAT? OPEN MY HOME?

But the six months we had planned on living there dragged into two-and-a-half long years. I never lifted a finger to make those dreary rooms attractive. In all that time, we invited only one couple from the university to come over and eat with us.

Though I studied cookbooks and experimented with recipes designed for a shoestring budget, I still doubted my ability to cook a "company" meal. I had ample reason to doubt—it seemed that every time I used the pressure cooker, it blew up.

LeRoy would help me scrape carrots, spinach, even bits of stewed chicken off the kitchen ceiling and walls, whenever the cooker blew its relief valve. If we had company for dinner, they might discover my kitchen clumsiness!

After LeRoy finished school, he accepted a job in Florida at the Kennedy Space Center. It was a booming area with housing as scarce as gold nuggets. Over the next several years we lived in a succession of dwellings: a postage stamp-size trailer, a cottage the owner braggingly said she'd converted from a chicken coop, and box-style houses in various subdivision tracts.

ASK JESUS "HOW?"

All this time I called myself a Christian, yet it never crossed my mind to ask Jesus how I could turn a chicken coop into a haven for my family. I was still pining for a dream house, one I could invite friends to share with us. In my mind's eye it was a four-bedroom, three-bath, ranch style brick house surrounded by lots of trees for our youngsters to climb—we had three children before the oldest was four. But this dream was both impractical and out of reach.

Then one day I stumbled on a way to be hospitable, almost by accident. We were new in town; we had three small children and were hungry for fellowship with other Christians.

We attended a church that was forming for the first time. Afterwards everyone stood around getting acquainted. A young woman named Lib Parker, who was just my age, suddenly said to me, "I wonder if you would like to go home, and get your Sunday dinner and bring it to our house. I know this is unusual, but we do not have enough for two families. I just think it would be great if our families could get to know one another."

I turned to LeRoy, and he answered for us: "Why not? Sounds like fun!"

So we went to Lib and Gene's house that Sunday; the next

Sunday they brought their four sons to our house—along with their dinner. During the following year we combined our Sunday dinners often, either at their small house or ours. Sometimes we picnicked at Fox Lake. The children played outdoors on swings in warm weather and huddled indoors over games in the cold winter months. Who enjoyed it the most, the children or the adults? Lib and I became longtime prayer partners; our children always felt they had four "Parker brothers."

MY CHANGED PERSPECTIVE

Before long, it dawned on me that I just might be able to adjust to my limitations and make better use of what we had in our home. Though I was still shy around people, I yearned to open my heart and home to others—to really "practice hospitality."

The art of hospitality comes naturally to some men and women, but it didn't for me. I had to get my feet wet in a tiny stream before I would be comfortable around others. I had to face the fact it is not so much what I cook on a limited budget, but that I prepare it with love.

I simply did not accept myself. I focused on all my "have-nots," never accepting any of my God-given "haves."

I finally got my perspective in the right place one morning when I was reading the Old Testament. Excitement raced through my heart when I read what God told his children living in exile:

> Build houses and settle down; plant gardens and eat what they produce.... Also, seek the peace and prosperity of the city to which I have carried you into exile. Pray to the Lord for it, because if it prospers, you too will prosper.
>
> Jeremiah 29:5, 7

Why, I was God's child. Even if I felt I was living in exile, I should act as if my home was permanent. I resolved to treat it with more imagination and love—and to share it with others. I prayed God would show me how.

CHRIST AT HOME IN MY HOME

The lessons were long and hard before I got my perspective straightened out. I knew that the more Christ was at home in my heart, the more he would be at home in my home. Right? That meant I would be glad to walk with him through every room of my house and have him sit at my table, too. I would not be ashamed for him to open any closet or listen in on our suppertime table talk. I would be thrilled for him to see into every nook and cranny of the home I lovingly made into a refuge for my family.

Invite him to open my cluttered closet? Invite him to eat any meal I cooked? Are you kidding?

Lib gave me a plaque: *Christ the unseen guest at our table.* Sometimes I regretted that I hung it on our kitchen wall. Was the conversation at our table pleasing to him? Or did I spend too much of mealtime fussing at the children? Or correcting them? Or maybe even passing on some gossip? Or complaining instead of counting my blessings?

My attitude began to change when I turned again to the Scriptures. In Luke 10:38 I found that Jesus enjoyed going to Bethany where "a woman named Martha opened her home to him." I'm sure it wasn't always convenient for her. When he came, twelve hungry men were tagging along!

A good portion of Jesus' ministry was home-centered. He said to a chief tax collector, "Zacchaeus, come down immediately. I must stay at your house today" (Lk 19:5b). When he went to Peter's home for supper, Jesus healed his mother-in-law of a fever, then she got up and served him.

Jesus enjoyed a wedding in Cana, a banquet at Simon's house, and a feast at Levi's. After he rose from the dead, he served a fish breakfast over a charcoal fire to his discouraged disciples on the sandy shores of the lake. I like to imagine him throwing the first "dinner on the grounds" party when he invited over five thousand to stay while he multiplied five fish and two loaves to feed them all. I think he was very much at home in Bethany with Lazarus and his sisters, Mary and Martha. He loved to go there—apparently he stayed with them whenever he was in the area. Hospitality was their lifestyle.

Not all of us were blessed to grow up in a family where hospitality was a lifestyle. But Laura (Watson) was o..e of those. She remembers during the Great Depression when her dad would bring one of his employees home for a good meal and a chance to air his problems. Laura's mother never knew how many mouths she would be feeding on any given evening, but somehow everybody always had enough.

Laura remembers, too, watching from the crack behind an open door while her mother and a friend knelt to pray for one another. This was also a common occurrence in their household.

One of her red-faced memories is when she was ten years old and determined to bake her daddy's birthday cake. It fell flat, and the fudge frosting was hard as a brick. It cracked into pieces when her daddy cut it. Worst of all, her Grandmother Anderson, who was known far and wide for her excellent cooking, was watching.

That trauma hounded her for years. When Laura married at nineteen, she was still unskilled at preparing a company meal alone. After many years of marriage, Laura and her husband, Brooks, struggled to fit "company for dinner" into their busy schedule—"I would rather have been doing something else!" she admits.

But when they built a new house seven years ago, they knew God wanted them to invite overnight—and sometimes "overweek"—guests. That meant decorating their guest room with special care—and cooking many meals!

"It has worked out beautifully. I'm convinced," Laura says firmly, "that God is directing all this, because the timing is always right. Even during periods like this past winter when there was someone staying overnight or longer at least once *every* week for five months. I have found that even when we have had a lot of company successively, there is always time available to relax, be quiet, and replenish our energy. Besides—we have hosted some fantastic people. I feel blessed to serve the Lord as I serve the people he sends our way."

A reminder of these "fantastic people" is the large quilt that hangs on the wall in Laura's guest room. When someone spends a night—or longer, Laura and Brooks ask them to autograph the quilt, then Laura embroiders over their names. This "guest book," with names ranging from their grandchildren to a journalist from India, missionaries to Peru, Nigeria, the Philippines, Rotarians from Sweden—and others—is a continual source of joy when the Watsons reflect on the blessings they have shared.

In *Disciplines of the Home*, Anne Ortlund says, "A Christian home is a powerful show-and-tell. Through the years Christian homes have won more Christian converts than all preachers and teachers put together."[1]

Laura and I want to encourage you to accept your home, wherever you live, under whatever circumstances, as the place God has provided for you for this time in your life. We're glad to see our children's generation is more resilient than ours. Sherry is now in her fifth year in Denmark. This week her brother, Keith, and his wife will visit her for the first time while on a business trip with Youth With a Mission's Mercy Ships.

Your home is God's provision for you. Whether you are married or single, it can be a source of blessing to others, whether you live alone or with others, your home can be a tool of ministry to other single adults, married couples, and families. Our God is a God of creativity, not limitation. He is not limited by our circumstances or our budgets or our personalities—and we should not feel limited by them either.

Prayer

Father, thank you for this place you have given me to live. I accept it and I give it back to you to do with as you please. Release your flow of creativity in me through my home as I use it as a tool of ministry to serve you, my family, and all you send my way.

2

My House—
Dream House
or Nightmare?

Unless the Lord builds the house, its builders labor in vain. **Psalm 127:1a**

"SAY, YOUR LIVING ROOM really has potential," Mary Jo Looney, a grandmother with a pixie smile, said as her eyes roamed across our living room. I had just finished teaching an informal Christian writing course at my house.

"What do you mean?" I asked, puzzled. I had met Mary Jo only once, but I heard she had a flair for decorating on a shoestring budget.

"Oh, if your furniture was arranged differently, you'd be able to seat more people in here."

"How?" I asked, skeptical. LeRoy and I had moved and reshuffled our den and living room furniture many times so we could accommodate up to twenty people who met twice a week for our Bible studies. But our current arrangement was the best possible, or so we thought.

Just a few weeks earlier I asked God for ways to express more imagination and love through my home. Now this virtual stranger who had been sitting in my living room for barely two hours was telling me it had potential!

Could she really arrange the furniture better? She was just a grandmother, with no professional credentials—only a gift of service.

She offered to bring some friends from her church over to give our whole house a facelift. Her stipulation: my husband had to agree. With LeRoy's consent, I invited her.

What did I need to do to get ready? First, I asked my prayer partner, Lib, to be there when this bevy of strangers invaded our home to do heaven-knows-what. The night before they came, I barely slept, worrying over whether I made a big mistake in giving Mary Jo carte blanche with my house. What if I didn't like what she did? What if I was really uncomfortable with her results?

She told me on the phone that God had already supplied what I needed for our home. Most women have accessories hidden in their closet, attic, garage, or under the bed. Mary Jo would look there for ours.

Not if I could help it! I did not want her clawing through my closets, let alone the garage. So I rummaged through things myself and pulled out all the extras I thought she might use, piling them on the picnic table on our screened porch. Besides, it would save her time as well as me embarrassment.

On Thursday morning Mary Jo arrived at our front door wearing a carpenter's apron complete with hammer and nails. She carried dried flowers and a large staple gun. She also was trailed by four women I had never met. "Meet our team," she said, calling off their names. "Now for Decorating Day—D-Day, we'll call it." She asked Lib and me to sit in the living room with them as they prayed before getting started on the renovation.

Lord, may your creative gifts flow through each of us, so that we may decorate this home to your glory. May it reflect the personality of the family that lives here—not our own individual tastes. Lord, we just want to make it an even more inviting place for Quin's family and all others who will come. Give us your strength and joy as we work together. When we leave, may even more of your peace pervade this home. We thank you for the privilege of helping each other, using the various talents you've given us. In Jesus' name, Amen.

After the prayer we all headed upstairs to the master bedroom. "Mary Jo," I protested, "you told me you would rearrange our living room so we could seat more people. Why in the world are you going to the master bedroom first?"

"Because the master bedroom should be the prettiest room in the house. That is the sanctuary for you and your husband—where the king and queen reside. Now get busy and clear this clutter—throw out these old magazines and other stuff you don't really need every day. Go down to your living room and bring me the most gorgeous bric-a-brac you have there."

"But you promised me the living room would..."

"By the end of the day, you will see that the living room will also look good, but this room where you and LeRoy spend your time together must be the most attractive, not just a room full of leftovers," Mary Jo explained as she made a shooing motion with her hands.

While she and a couple of her friends rearranged the furniture upstairs, Margaret was busy making curtains from printed sheets for our bedroom windows.

Our oldest daughter, Quinett, who was taking sewing in high school, helped Margaret sew up curtains for her own three bedroom windows from pink and blue flowered sheets. Margaret showed her how to use the heavy-duty staple gun to cover the wall behind her bed with matching sheet fabric. It looked better than any fancy wallpaper.

Keith's room got a blue theme, and I told him he could paint a surfing scene across one whole wall that weekend.

Sherry's room was redone in yellow flowered sheets—-curtains, bedspread, lampshade, canopy over the bed and one wall, all covered in matching fabric.

Meanwhile I kept busy polishing old brass pieces that Mary Jo wanted for wall decorations and running up and down the stairs to deliver supplies to various ones who called for help. Once in a while I peeked in to see how Mary Jo and Lib were doing with the den or kitchen furniture.

It was a good thing I committed this day's activities to the Lord, or I would have been upset when I saw them switching furniture from room to room. But I remembered our prayer that morning, and I knew God was using his creativity in each woman.

I could hardly believe the great new look they were creating, using what we already had to better advantage. In fact, they were capturing our family's personality in the minute details, even in what they chose to use in wall groupings, from family pictures to my grandmother's antique china plate from England.

I had often complained about our old furniture as "those awful hand-me-downs," since much of what we owned were relatives' cast-offs or used-furniture-store bargains. But now, in their new places near windows, those wonderful old wood grains shone as the sunlight bounced off them.

Mary Jo was true to her promise in the living room. When she rearranged the couch, chairs, and end tables, we had more than ample room for our Bible study crowd.

Late that night as I collapsed in bed, tired but happy, I thought back over the day. I recognized that no matter where I ever moved again—to a walk-up flat, a crude beach cottage, a cabin in the woods—it would be home. Our spot. Our place to express our likes, tastes, personalities.

AN EXAMPLE TO QUINETT

This truth came back to me a couple of years later when we took Quinett off to college. As soon as the university president got parents and freshmen gathered for orientation, he told the students bluntly, "Your dorm room is going to be your home for the next four years. So accept it." It pleased me to hear him tell these eighteen-year-olds what it had taken me so long to learn.

I jabbed an elbow in Quinett's side. "Honey, he didn't have to tell you that. You brought everything you own. Surely this will be home," I said, laughing quietly with her.

She had literally moved out of our house—bag and baggage. Inside I was sad—that empty nest syndrome—seeing all her belongings piled up in the middle of a dorm room. But I knew she was in good shape because she had already accepted it in advance; by using what she had to work with, she had made plans to turn this into the prettiest, coziest room possible.

Standing there with sheets draped over my arms, I watched Quinett show me how she planned to make them into curtains for her long narrow windows. I couldn't help but think back to the many places where I lived over the years. I resolved once again that in whatsoever house I am, therewith I will be content. I will not only be content, I will do everything I can to make it a pretty, comfortable, and appealing home for me and my family. Only in God's will does a house become a home. Creating a home is possible whether you are single like my daughter or married like me. Any dwelling becomes a home where love is creatively displayed and people are lovingly served.

CLEARING THE CLUTTER

Mary Jo later taught a class I attended on homemaking to the church women, and started out with a stunning question:

"Are you the best housekeeper you know how to be?" Opening her Bible, she read, "And whatever you do, whether in word or deed, do it all in the name of the Lord Jesus, giving thanks to God the Father through him" (Col 3:17).

While women squirmed in discomfort, she made another

appalling statement: "God sees into closets, too!" I did not like that! I am just not neat, I thought to myself. But I kept listening.

"God is a God of order, not confusion, and everything should be kept in its proper place. Look at how beautiful and orderly he made the universe. He planned seasons of the year. God wants our homes to reflect the same order he puts in nature—organized and attractive."

I noticed some of the other women also shifting in their seats, as she continued.

"We can get so wrapped up in habit we are blinded by clutter. I'm sure none of you leaves your ironing board piled so high with clothes that your husband has to step over it to get into bed. None of you parks your vacuum cleaner in the living room and lets it stay there for decoration," she said, eyebrows raised. Some women giggled, identifying their own poor housekeeping habits.

Here is the list of suggestions she gave us that day:

- The master bedroom should be the prettiest in the house—keep it picked up and orderly. Whether you are single or married, make your bedroom the most attractive room, because you want to create order and peace in the decor of your special place.
- The children's room should be next in importance. Make them feel special. Help them pick the colors, wall hangings and some Scripture plaques. Spend money on good mattresses for them.
- The dining room or kitchen is next in importance, wherever the family sits to eat and enjoy family fellowship.
- If you are married, have a special "hubby" corner for your husband—his place to feel at home.
- The living room, or whatever room is used when company is entertained, is lower on the priority list because family comes first. But it is still important because it witnesses to others of your commitment to God by your orderliness.

- In each room ask yourself, "Is Jesus pleased with this room?" If not, discard the things you would not want him to see. Disorder? Rearrange the room.
- Keep the house clutter-free. Get rid of outdated catalogs, old magazines, shoes and clothes that don't fit. Remember this Scripture: "A time to keep, and a time to throw away" (Eccl 3:6b).
- Go through one room at a time—do a thorough job of each one before going on to the next. Set a goal: one chest of drawers today... one closet tomorrow... one bookcase the next day. It will overwhelm and discourage you if you try to do too much at one time.
- At night before going to bed, straighten your living room and kitchen. What a relief to come to breakfast without having to face a mess!

After I shared with my friend Pat what Mary Jo had taught me about decorating, she wrote me:

I came home, and two days later began to rearrange a room of furniture, using "new" decorations from storage in my attic. Now I find myself just sitting in that room to read at odd moments in the day. It's like a brand new place. My husband enjoys it also. My plan is to move through my house, one room at a time, making changes without spending money!

HOME-MAKERS

Down the street from us, a nurse had an apartment so crowded with gifts from grateful patients that she had to crawl over the piles of stuff to get into her bed. One day she loaded her car with items she could not use and carted them off to a nursing home. Though each gift had been given to her with love, she chose to freely share them with others. Her apartment is now attractive and comfortable—and uncluttered.

Once LeRoy and I visited a middle-aged Christian couple we barely knew. We squirmed our way past laundry baskets and an ironing board piled high with wrinkled clothes—in the living room. Magazines were carelessly strewn on the floor beside the chairs. Books were lying helter-skelter everywhere, on tables, chairs, and the floor. In the front yard an old boat with peeling paint stood as an eyesore that certainly said anything but "welcome" to the home. It was not that they were dirty or uncaring. They just became careless about the way they lived since there were only two of them left at home.

When they were invited for fellowship in other Christian homes, they came face-to-face with their own bad habits. They went home and organized their house's clutter. The next time we visited them, I could hardly believe it was the same home.

Annette, a widow, says that since the Lord promised to be her husband when she lost hers (Is 54:5), she keeps her master bedroom the prettiest room in the house. "It is my sanctuary. That is where I usually pray the most as the Lord and I have long talks. I enjoy the beauty of it, and I know the Lord honors the fact that it is not messy but orderly."

All these have discovered, as I have, that it is Jesus who makes the difference. Just as Jesus clears the clutter from our lives when we become his, so our homes should be cleared of clutter to reflect his presence. Only he can turn house-keepers into home-makers.

3

Decorating on
a Tight Budget

*But everything should be done in a fitting and orderly
way.*   1 Corinthians 14:40

WHAT DOES DECORATING have to do with hospitality? Think
a moment. Don't you feel more comfortable having others
in when your home is picked up, orderly? I believe that before
we can be hospitable, we have to feel "at home" in our home.

"Christian hospitality is not a matter of money, age, social
standing, or personality. It is a matter of obedience to God,"
writes Helga Henry.[1]

Vivian Hall, in *Be My Guest*, says hospitality is easier when we
live by these simple rules:

- Decide on the lifestyle that is best for you (and your family
  if you have one) and live accordingly.

- Live within your means. Finances, time, and energy are limited commodities, so do not overextend yourself in a desire to make a good impression.
- Be adaptable.
- Eliminate competition from your relationships with other people. Seek to gain the approval of God and not that of men.[2]

BE YOURSELF

To her list I added:

- Be yourself! Each of us is unique, with a variety of gifts and personalities. Let your home reflect yours. Start with things you treasure and build from there.

That is how Laura set the theme for her home office, her special space in their new house. The Watsons were getting ready to move from a house they had lived in for fourteen years, so a lot of time was spent sorting through the accumulation of stored stuff. But it gave her an opportunity to discover creative new uses for old treasures.

While packing the contents of the closet, she found a dried sprig of hyssop and a poppy she had pressed in her Bible from a trip to Israel seven years before. Sitting back on her heels on the floor of the near-empty room, she saw two matching picture frames she had saved "because they were too good to throw away." They were just right to display these small symbols of God's care. Hyssop was used in Old Testament times for purification—it told Laura it was time to clean up, get organized. The poppy was a reminder of Jesus' words to "Consider the lilies of the field" (Mt 6:28 RSV) and how he would care for her needs, too.

Other items that surfaced that day were odds and ends of knitting yarn. She selected a blue strand to tie a bow on the hyssop and a pale peach one for the poppy. Framed, they were the first things she hung above the desk in her new office—things made out of "findings" that were there all the time.

In fact, these two cherished items set the theme for the room's colors. Laura had an old sofa covered in a pale green (matching the green from the hyssop), with a splashy print for chair, valance, and toss pillows that incorporates the dull red of the dried poppy, the same french blue of one of the yarn scraps and a background of the pale peach of the other yarn bow.

DECOR PLEASING TO THE LORD

My own experience was a change of attitude, when I realized that everything I have belongs to God. I did some soul searching. If my home was his, did I have it—and myself—arranged to please my family as well as the Lord?

Mary Jo teaches that our entryway should exalt Jesus so whenever anyone comes in, they will know Jesus lives there too. One day when our paperboy came to collect, he asked me, "Why is your manger scene sitting out here in August?" I replied, "It reminds me year round that God sent his Son into the world to show us what God is like. Do you know Jesus?" It was a perfect opportunity for witnessing. So now I leave it on the hall table all year round.

Pastor Peter Lord encouraged us to make Scripture plaques for the entryways to our homes. He made one for his wife: "Johnnie, you are a wife of noble character worth far more than rubies" (Prv 31:10). Ready-made Scripture plaques are available at most Christian bookstores.

In his colorful book, *Interior Decorating: a Reflection of the Creator's Design*, Georg Andersen says that the key to an effective entrance area is not the design scheme. "It is you. You must be, as Paul wrote, 'given to hospitality' (Rom 12:13)." Unless you show yourself warm and friendly, your guests will never feel welcome, no matter how inviting the wallpaper or warm the lighting."[3]

Ponder that as you think of building your own room—or house—scheme. You will no doubt be troubled by, "If I could just get a new chair... or sofa... or table..." That may well be the only way to pull your room together. However, look first at your purpose, then at the things you can do to "make do" with what you have. You may be surprised at what is at hand, just as Laura was.

ADAPT OR ADOPT

But, you say, what will I do with that old table that just gets in the way because it does not go with anything? This may be just the right time to store it, donate it to a charity, or have a garage sale.

I read in a good book on decorating: "Consider what you like about the furnishings you've kept—bright colors, perhaps, or natural materials. Look for new pieces that will fit in or will provide the one striking accent that could make the whole room special."[4]

Jackie bought a new sofa and curtains for their vacation cottage, and the budget would not stretch any further. Looking around, a friend who visited her there noticed the green and beige plaid afghan that coordinated with the sofa. "Why don't we drape it over that awful yellow and brown chair? It would hide the places where the stuffing is oozing out." The tight budget was forgotten as they congratulated each other on their creativity.

Must you really have a new table? Take the Lord shopping with you. Have you looked at garage sales, flea markets, second-hand stores? If you find just the right piece except for the terrible condition of its finish, there are products in any hardware store that will help you refinish furniture.

Does your color scheme need a facelift? Decorators have noticed that peach and pink tones appear to make women's skin glow (and it probably has a similar effect on men's skin). That would be a good way to highlight the self-esteem of your guests. Try it in the living room or guest room. They will love it, and so will you. Or you might want to "white out" your mistakes—paint everything in sight white: walls, ceilings, paneling, even brick fireplaces, as well as a few pieces of furniture. It makes a bright, cheerful and neutral backdrop for colorful accessories and is a way to blend different furniture styles.

Then give your room warmth with books, baskets, flowers, candles. There are a number of ways to highlight favorite items that will say "this is my room." There is more impact and less clutter when small collectibles are displayed together. With candles, be sure when they are lit the flame is above or below eye level to avoid glare.

The mystery of mixing patterns in fabric is easy to solve—just vary the size of the patterns used within a room. Stripes and plaids in coordinating colors add vigor to a predominantly floral scheme. If you are using mostly solid colors, consider the texture. All flat weaves can be boring—nubby or damask weaves add character.

CHRISTIAN SYMBOLS

As LeRoy and I longed to reflect more of Jesus—after we invited him into our lives and home—we looked for ways to do it. At an art show we found our first decorative piece that expressed our faith: a handcrafted bronze and wood plaque with a cross superimposed over a fish and the word "Savior" engraved underneath. We hung it inside our front entrance.

Christian symbols used to turn me off. I would go into a home and see a profusion of plaster plaques and something inside me would churn. I was not walking with Jesus then and did not know the significance of the emblems.

Later when I came to understand their meanings, I realized our home could be tastefully decorated with emblems of our faith without splashing the walls and coffee table with cheap objets d'art. I also wanted to guard against a hodge-podge effect.

I am sure there are others who still don't care for symbolism, perhaps fearing it borders on idolatry. Yet our Christian faith is rich in symbolism. Jesus referred to himself as the Bread of Life, the True Vine, the Light of the World.

Of all Christian symbols, the cross is perhaps the most universally accepted today. More than four hundred shapes are in existence, including the Latin, Greek, Jerusalem, Celtic, and Maltese crosses.

The empty cross in our entry hall constantly reminds us of a Savior who conquered death and now lives. The fish sign is also of special significance.

Early Christians used a simple fish design as a symbol for "Savior." The Greek word for fish, pronounced IKTHUS, formed a rebus with the following meaning:

> Jesus
> Christ
> God's
> Son
> Savior

It was a secret sign of identity. They drew the fish emblem on the doorposts of the homes and in the catacombs where they met for worship. Though Christians in our country do not have to meet in secret, many have an IKTHUS (fish) posted on their front door, identifying themselves with the Lord Jesus.

We discovered in our family's reading that communion provided one of the original symbols of the Christian faith. The church "signed its name" by chiseling the symbol of the bread and the cup into stone or by painting it on walls.

On our kitchen wall we hung a picture which shows a cup of wine, a loaf of bread and a printed invitation:

JESUS OF NAZARETH
Requests the Honor
Of Your Presence
At a Dinner
To Be Given in His Honor

CLEAR THE CLUTTER

After we invited Jesus into our lives, we asked him to show us what we needed to remove from our home. "Lord Jesus, is there anything in here that is an abomination to you? Anything that is connected with the occult or the demonic realm?"

We got rid of face masks from the West Indies, Greek souvenirs with mythical goddesses on them, a world map with astrological signs around it, an Indian painting and other wall hangings that missionary friends told us had Hindu deities on them. Souvenir dishes that pictured Roman gods were thrown away.

God's warning to the Israelites is as appropriate today as then: "The images of their gods you are to burn in the fire. Do not covet the silver and gold on them, and do not take it for yourselves, or you will be ensnared by it..." (Dt 7:25).

Deuteronomy 18:9-14 declares that occult activity is an abomination to God. Such activity includes astrology (reading horoscopes), palm reading, ouija boards, Tarot cards, seances, fortune telling, witchcraft, divination, sorcery, magic, casting spells or hexes, and more.

I asked the Lord to forgive me for innocently having objects in our home that would be abominable to him. And I looked for ways to exhibit tasteful symbols of Christianity.

I began to notice ways others reflected Christ in their decorating schemes:

- In the gable above the front porch of the Buckinghams' house, there is the cutout of a dove, symbol of the Holy Spirit. Lit from behind with a blue bulb, its glow tells all who come up the driveway that God's Spirit rests on this house.

- In Sarah's entryhall, her great-grandmother's well-worn Bible is open and resting on a handcarved wooden stand.
- Joy's living room pillows are needlepoint designs of biblical scenes.
- The focal point of Linda's dining room is an oil painting of Bethlehem done by Frank, her artist husband.
- Lib leaves small devotional books in her guest room and bath.
- An inexpensive stained glass Bible scene hangs in Jo's living room.
- Laura's den bookshelves are tastefully interspersed with dainty angel figurines. She also has a painting in her entry of a vision of angels she once had—but the focal point of the picture—as of the vision—is the light of the Holy Spirit portrayed in a cross of light in the upper lefthand corner. People who come into the entry often comment on the unusual painting, and that gives Laura an opening to share the love of the Lord.

Millie Lyon, a missionary in the jungles of Peru, says, "I use lots of plants, some pictures, some conversation pieces, and keep it all simple. Comfort to Floyd and me means fans, toss pillows, uncluttered areas, and a relaxed attitude. A few well-placed family pictures are interesting, because everyone has family. Several pictures of the Indians we work with bring on a discussion of why we live in Peru. Bright colors with lots of the outdoors showing from our living room windows reminds us of God's creation."

COUNT THE COST

A California mother with three toddlers lived on a houseboat to please her husband, an unbeliever, while he was gone almost nine months of the year on Navy duty. "I decided that instead of grumbling about my circumstances, it would be a better witness to Jesus if I accepted that houseboat as home and made better use of what space I did have. It was worth it. My show of love was not wasted—he knew I did it to make him happy," she told me.

Hospitality will cost you. Jesus said to follow him, but he also said to count the cost. Couches will tear, chairs will break, carpet will stain. But whose is it? It belongs to God. We know anything material will deteriorate.

I remember well one night when I came close to missing God's best for me in this area.

As the prayer meeting at our house ended, Pastor Peter Lord hurriedly snapped his briefcase shut. "Hate to leave so soon, but I have a plane to catch tonight," he said, walking toward the front door. When he reached the front hall, we noticed ink spewing from the sides of his closed briefcase. Almost the entire length of our living room was sprinkled with big black drops.

He apologized profusely. "It is all right, Peter. You are forgiven. We will get it up," I said as I ushered him out the door. LeRoy and I and a few others grabbed some towels and set to work on our hands and knees trying to sop up ink blobs.

When I was blotting the stains right in front of the coffee table, I suddenly remembered this was the exact spot where I knelt almost four years earlier when we dedicated our home to the Lord. Here I had turned this house (and everything in it) over to him, acknowledging that I was only a caretaker of it.

Now I relaxed. "Forgive me, Lord. I forgot for a moment. This is your carpet, so it is your problem. How do we get it clean?"

When I looked up and saw Lillie still rocking in her chair, I was frustrated. Why wasn't she helping us? "She's your intercessor," God's still small voice told me. "Sorry, I forgot," I replied.

Abruptly she said, "Get some milk." We did, and sponged it over the ink spots. God's carpet came clean.

I was so proud of myself. I had forgiven the pastor, God had cleaned the carpet, and I was praising him for a job well done. Then I realized I had no room for pride—God had put Lillie, his intercessor, there. God cares about spots on carpet.

God will provide when couches wear out... when food is needed... when time is short, if we will just trust him.

OTHER SUGGESTIONS

Need help in personalizing your home? Mary Jo has decorated more than one thousand homes free of charge. She believes in sharing what you don't need. Anything that is not needed after a house's transformation, is recycled. First it goes into Mary Jo's "goody van." The next home she goes into may need that very lamp, bedspread, or curtains. For example, in the Baptist pastor's kitchen are curtains that once hung in a Presbyterian elder's bedroom. When Mary Jo taught a women's seminar, she shared a list of household suggestions, some hers, some gleaned from others.

1. If you need a buffet server in the dining room, consider moving a long dresser from a bedroom to the dining area. After all, a chest is a chest is a chest. Use it where you need it most. If you move it from a bedroom, it might provide room for a chair or desk in that bedroom.
2. Don't hang pictures too high. Eye level is best. Hang pictures and mirrors off-center, and use groupings over couches and beds. Don't be afraid to experiment. If you goof and need to hide a small nail hole in the wall, toothpaste will cover it.
3. Give a personal touch to the hallway by hanging family portraits.
4. Frame Scripture verses, postcards, and unusual greeting cards for wall decor. Mary Jo believes in putting Scripture verse plaques in every room of the house. "Change them

often in the bathroom—you have a captive audience there, and kids will memorize them painlessly," she laughed.

5. Paint a family tree (literally a tree, with trunk and graceful branches). Hang framed family pictures on them.

6. Hang a small picture inside built-in bookcases.

7. Put chairs in bedrooms so people have a place to sit to read or visit. If the room is large enough, group two chairs with a small table and lamp for a sitting-room effect. This is especially good for the master bedroom.

8. A dust ruffle sewn to a fitted sheet keeps the ruffle from sliding off-center.

9. Cover window shades: cut to fit fabric that coordinates with the bedspread, then glue on with spray adhesive.

10. Make curtain tiebacks from ribbon, yarn, boat rope, chains, braids, beads, or a contrasting fabric ruffle.

11. Make headboards out of anything interesting. One of our friends made a headboard for their king-size bed from an old archway of a building that was being demolished.

12. Marbelize a table top by painting it a cream color; let dry. Wipe a coat of oil base stain across it, then lay a sheet of saran wrap on top; lift off immediately—marble!

13. Don't be afraid to mix periods of furniture. Most will blend harmoniously if you don't go overboard.

14. Make matching bedspread and curtains from decorative sheets. Staple sheets on a wall behind your bed for an interesting and colorful effect.

15. Sew lace doilies or hankies onto solid color toss pillows. This looks especially elegant on a velvet pillow.

16. Keep glass, silver, and brass clean and polished. It reflects light and creates an atmosphere of warmth. Use rubbing alcohol to clean glass, chrome, and the shower stall—even black shoe polish from carpet!

17. Dried flowers or weeds look great in tall or small baskets, and they keep indefinitely. However, be sure to spray weeds with a bug killer before bringing them indoors. To keep weeds from shedding, spray with hair spray.

18. A live potted plant, a dry arrangement, or silk flowers in each room (including baths) will bring subtle colors of nature into your home.

A PLACE OF YOUR DREAMS

Mary Crowley, in *Decorate Your Home With Love,* writes: "Rooms that say, 'Welcome—snuggle down and stay awhile! People live here who laugh and hug and listen to each other's problems. Who care and share and have a good time.' It is a feeling of harmony, caring, friendliness, fun. It is done by 'decorating'—and you can do it too!"[5]

Home can be a place of your dreams only if you're willing to put yourself into it. But how fulfilling it is when you hear your family and friends say, "I feel comfortable in this place." And you hear the Lord say, "Well done, thou good and faithful servant."

4

Learn
to Receive

Therefore receive one another, just as Christ also received us, to the glory of God. **Romans 15:7 NKJV**

W E WERE ALL TAUGHT that "It is more blessed to give than to receive." But somehow in our spiritual thinking, we've got it all out of kilter. Where is the balance between giving and receiving?

To begin with, our attitude in giving sets the tone for the other person's comfort in receiving.

One night after a women's meeting, Laura looked up to see her friend Wylene walking toward her with a paper sack. What was she up to now? With a mischievous grin, Wylene said, "Hold out your hand. I want to give you something no one has ever given you at this church." She put a fresh egg in Laura's open palm: "This one is for you"; another, "and this one is for your husband"; and a third, "and this one is for your son."

Crazy. Eggs? As a gift?

But Laura felt special. Yes, the fresh eggs tasted good for breakfast the next morning. But the real gift was that she was accepted—Wylene knew Laura would respond with delight at her outlandish sense of humor. And Laura knew that Wylene knew, because they are friends.

This incident must fit that category where the Bible says, "God loveth a cheerful giver." I am told the word translated as "cheerful" there literally means "hilarious."

Since we are Jesus' friends, he must be delighted too when we give with that kind of hilarious abandon. Whether it is money, time, talents—or fresh eggs.

Why do we resist receiving? Is it because we feel unworthy? Of course we are. But Jesus died for us, so he considers us more precious than his own life. If we don't receive Jesus, there really isn't any meaning in giving presents to others at Christmas as a celebration of his birth.

The reason I can open my home so freely to others is because I learned to ask for help. The first time I had forty people coming over for supper, I thought I could handle it myself. However, I soon found that was ridiculous. I called Lib, and she came running over—in her bedroom slippers. Many times since then when I had a big party, Lib would be in the kitchen doing the punch, replenishing the sandwiches. I called her my Martha.

MY LESSON IN RECEIVING

Let me tell you how I learned my biggest lesson in receiving from others. Our family of five had just sat down in the dining room for supper when the doorbell rang. "I'll get it," twelve-year-old Keith said, dashing to the door.

He came back more slowly, carefully carrying a bouquet of pastel spring flowers. He handed me the accompanying card. I glanced at LeRoy who was trying to hide a smug smile.

"With love from your sweetheart, LeRoy," I read aloud.

"Wow, Dad must have done something awful! Flowers? For no special occasion, Mom?" Keith asked.

"Of course it isn't a special occasion, honey. But aren't they pretty?"

Fifteen years earlier, on our first anniversary, LeRoy had sent me a dozen red roses. But none since then. What had he done? What had I done? Why flowers?

The next night as we sat down to eat, LeRoy slipped a brightly wrapped present from under the table and put it beside my plate. Surprised, I opened it to find a new nightgown. A love note was tucked into its folds.

The following evening he offered to do the dishes. The next night he volunteered to vacuum the downstairs. Since he was not accustomed to doing either, I brushed him off. "Are you kidding? Go read your newspaper. This is my job."

"Friday night I would like to take you to Sandpiper's, the finest seafood restaurant on the east coast. Be ready at six, dressed in your best," he said firmly.

"But it's the end of the month," I sputtered. "You know perfectly well we don't have enough money left to eat there. We can't possibly afford it!"

"Be ready. I'm taking my bride out for the night of her life."

The next morning I phoned my prayer partner, Lib. "LeRoy is acting strange. I wonder if I have reason to suspect him of something? I mean, he never offers to vacuum or wash dishes. And he sent flowers and gave me a gift for no particular reason. I tell you, something is fishy..."

"Oh, it's just a mid-life crisis!" Lib offered. No help at all.

On Saturday night I dressed in my best pink chiffon and reluctantly got in the car with LeRoy. En route to the restaurant he explained he had a tool that he must return to James England. He motioned toward the gadget on the seat between us.

Detouring, we drove up to the Englands' house. "Honey, get

out and go in with me," he urged. "Just for a minute."

"No way. The pastor's car is in the driveway. He's probably stopped by to pray with them. You know Ann is still in bed flat on her back, trying not to miscarry again."

"Come on. Please. Come on in just for a moment," LeRoy insisted.

I jumped out and walked up to the front door with LeRoy clutching the tool in his hand. He pressed the doorbell.

James flung open the door to welcome us. I could see a huge banner on the wall behind him: "WIVES, WE APPRECIATE YOU!"

In the next room I could see the pastor and his wife, Johnnie, watching. We all exploded in laughter. They told me that each of the eight husbands in our couples' group, which Pastor Peter Lord taught on Sunday evenings, had agreed to surprise his wife that week with flowers, a nightgown, and offers to help around the house.

Now the men were cooking us a scrumptious charcoal-grilled steak supper. Festive tables were set up in the dining and living rooms, complete with linen cloths and soft candlelight. Violinists had been hired to serenade us while we ate. The setting was far superior to the Sandpiper, and the food was certainly more delectable. One couple took their plates to join Ann and James in the bedroom since she couldn't leave the bed.

After dinner we played games, laughing uproariously. But our hilarity calmed considerably when Pastor Lord called timeout for his weekly questions and answers. Actually, it was his "report card time," since he graded us each week on how well we'd learned any lesson God was trying to teach us.

"What did you think when your husbands surprised you with gifts and offers to help?" he asked the wives. "How did you react? Were you a loving receiver?"

Each wife painfully agreed she deserved a big fat F (for failure) when it came to receiving graciously from her husband. We had all been highly suspicious, extremely poor receivers.

A few husbands got some low scores—LeRoy among them— for giving their wives flannel granny gowns instead of something beautiful and romantic.

I came away from that evening determined to be a good receiver. I have always found it easier to give than to receive, so I knew I would have to ponder this lesson repeatedly.

Hasn't God said he loves a cheerful giver... that it is more blessed to give than to receive? Hasn't he said, "Freely you have received, freely give"? True!

He also said, "Give, and it shall be given unto you; good measure, pressed down, and shaken together, and running over, shall men give into your bosom" (Lk 6:38a KJV).

GIVING RESTORES

Gradually I learned to find pleasure in doing, giving, and surprising others—but I was not prepared to be on the receiving end. The night of our wives' appreciation dinner, I finally understood that if my husband or friends wanted to give to me, I was robbing them of a blessing, a joy, and an opportunity by my negative attitude that said, "No, thank you. I don't need your gifts, talents, help..." At the same time, God was saying to me, "You are robbing yourself of the restorative quality of receiving."

You cannot be fulfilled by giving alone; it must be coupled with receiving, or you will soon be depleted—your desire to "give" will become superficial. You cannot give out of emptiness—you would only be calling attention to your need for approval.

On the other hand, taking in but never releasing becomes a stagnant state. Fatness is unhealthy as well as unbecoming.

Keep in mind that receiving honors the giver; refusal denies his personhood. Giving then draws the receiver into an inner circle of acceptance.

LEARNING THE HARD WAY

Dorothy and her husband Ronnie were accustomed to giving abundantly. If they heard of someone in financial trouble, or if someone needed counseling, they rushed to help. Their home was open once a week for a Bible study.

Then one spring, after twenty-one years at the same job, Ronnie was laid off. Dorothy kept teaching second grade even after her eyesight grew so poor that she could no longer drive.

The weeks stretched into almost a year-and-a-half. Doors to other jobs slammed closed in Ronnie's face. When they had a specific financial need, they wrote the exact amount in their little looseleaf prayer books. They never told anyone else about it. They just trusted God.

One week Dorothy wrote "$40" in her book for a household item that needed repair. Ronnie wrote "$70" in his book for something he needed in the house. Before the week was up, two checks were given to them which made up the exact amount they needed.

During this time they were sensitive to God's leading if they were to share something given to them with someone else. Once they shared money they had just received with two men. Later they learned that one man had needed an eye examination, the other had a car insurance payment due. "We were just channels for God's money, letting it come to us and through us," Dorothy delightedly explained.

They had learned the reality of "Give, and it will be given to you" (Lk 6:38a). So this couple, generous givers, learned to be gracious receivers.

A GIFT IS A GIFT

Margaret really has a handle on what it means to give. We call her the "bestest" breadmaker in town, because she often surprises her friends with her fresh-from-the-oven whole wheat loaves of goodness.

Margaret told me, "I once had the privilege of giving a loaf of bread to my friend Gladys. Then she had the privilege of giving it to someone else. We both got a blessing in giving." Then she smiled. "Don't ever forget, a gift is a gift is a gift. With no strings attached."

SURPRISE BLESSINGS

When we began taking young people into our home, a minister told us, "God will bless you." But I was not looking for any spectacular out-of-the-ordinary happening.

Then about six weeks later, LeRoy came in from work with a wide grin on his face and a blue check in his hand. "Guess what, honey? You are going to get a new kitchen for Christmas—at least a new oven and flooring for this room. See this?"

"What are you talking about? Where did you get that check?" I asked, sitting down to take in this sudden news.

"Well, you know each year they give special awards at work. I told the men in our carpool months ago that if I ever got one, it would be a miracle of God. I never expected it to happen. But look—a miracle in my hand!"

You can say LeRoy's company gave us that money, and you'd be right. But I believe God let them channel his money to us through that award—the first my husband had ever received in his twenty years with the company. Yes, God gave us a new oven for better meals and a new floor which takes less time to clean. I firmly believe what the minister told us came true. God poured out his blessings beyond measure after we received Mike into our home in Jesus' name, without thought of getting in return.

Laura and Brooks can identify with this principle. They had gone through a tough year when Brooks' business was about to fold, and their electric bill was due on Monday—but there was no money to pay it. They went to church on Sunday morning with heavy hearts, but they prayed that God would provide—he had never let them down yet.

When they came home (this was in the days when you could leave your front door unlocked in their small town), there on a chair in the living room was a check for $117—exactly the amount of the bill. It had been put there by a man whom Brooks had counseled and subsequently loaned money to nearly five years before (and then forgot about it). So they could rejoice not only that their need was supplied, but that their friend was trustworthy and was obviously prospering also.

PRECIOUS GIFTS

Reading my Bible, I am amazed to find how many guests mentioned there carried precious gifts with them, which they revealed to receptive hosts. Hospitable folk got blessings galore, without expecting anything.

When Abraham and Sarah received the three strangers at Mamre and offered them food, the Lord revealed through them that Sarah would have a son.

When Elijah, God's servant, asked the impoverished widow of Zarephath for water and bread at the moment she was preparing her last bit for her son and herself, she fed Elijah first. Then her bowl of flour and jar of oil never ran out during the long drought that followed.

When the prominent woman of Shunem and her husband built Elisha a room to stay in and gave him food, she was rewarded with the birth of a son.

Boaz offered bread and grain to Ruth, and got a wife in return; from their heirs came Jesus.

Though Abigail's husband, Nabal, was rich, he was an ill-mannered, selfish drunkard. She, on the other hand, was beautiful, intelligent, and hospitable. Saul was still on a rampage seeking David and his band of men—for David had already been anointed king by the prophet Samuel. During sheep-shearing time, as David and his men hid from Saul, he sent word to the wealthy Nabal asking for food. David's men reminded Nabal's men that they had been as a wall of protection around Nabal's huge flock of sheep and goats while out in the fields near Carmel. But Nabal refused bread, water, and meat for the future King David. When Abigail heard that her husband had declined hospitality, she took off on a donkey caravan to feed David's entourage. Sending her young men ahead, she met David on her way. Not only was she bearing food, she was also on an even more serious mission. Appealing to his conscience, she asked David not to be a murderer—not to kill her husband and bring a reproach upon David's own life. Later God himself killed Nabal.

When the two travelers to Emmaus invited the stranger walking on the road with them to stay for the night, Jesus made himself known to them in the breaking of the bread.

Look how Mary and Martha were blessed by having Jesus in their home. When their brother Lazarus died, Jesus came to Bethany to raise him from the grave and to reveal some of his greatest truths: "Martha, I am the resurrection and the life."

Who can ever forget the story of Jesus cooking breakfast for his disciples over a charcoal fire? When the disciples came up out of their boats, they saw him on the shore, a fire kindled, frying fish. "Now come and have some breakfast," he called to them. Then he, the Son of God, went around serving them bread and fish. And what of the disciples who had denied him, deserted him, failed him? They got a blessing that has reverberated through the tunnel of time. For in these precious intimate moments, they saw him for who he really is: the resurrected Lord, Son of God, Prince of Peace.

In this picture we see Jesus as both a giver and a receiver. He gives of himself in the serving. But he receives in welcoming his men—those friends who had failed him. He, the giver and the receiver, wants both from us.

So we can see the balance between giving and receiving is to temper mercy with wisdom, or a show of love will simply degenerate into sentimentality. Our need: for God's wisdom in each situation—-to be able to see through his eyes. Then the love I give will be God's love, and no one can resist that!

PART TWO

Blessings of a Family

5

Family
First

Now be pleased to bless the house of your servant, that it may continue forever in your sight.   2 Samuel 7:29a

MY SON KEITH hurried through my home office on his way to the kitchen for a drink. Seeing a magazine on my desk with my byline on an article, he stopped and picked it up. "By Quin Sherrer, Homemaker," he read aloud.

"Mom, I didn't know you were a homemaker," he said, looking me in the eye. "I just thought you were a writer."

"A writer? Not a homemaker? Oh... Keith!"

After he returned to his football game in the backyard, I fell across my typewriter and wept to the Lord.

"Lord, show me how to let them know I really am a homemaker and that they are the priority in my life," I prayed.

Leaving my typewriter, I went into the kitchen and started

supper. I prepared something that was "special" to each of our family members. That night when they came in, I had a starched tablecloth on the dining table. Candles were flickering; hot steaming bowls of chicken, mashed potatoes, and all the trimmings made the meal look mighty inviting.

"What is this?" Sherry asked. "I can't see with just candlelight."

"Honey, you will have to get used to it. God showed me—through Keith—that I haven't let you know that you are more important to me than any company that will ever sit in this room. I am sorry I haven't let you know you hold first place in my heart and life."

"Well, this is really a switch," Keith said.

LeRoy just nodded, knowingly.

I noticed that, as we ate night after night in the dining room with a nice cloth on the table and candles with a centerpiece, we were lingering longer and longer to talk—and to laugh.

I never bought fine china—just continued to use my all-white dishes and my stainless flatware. But at least we were not eating in the kitchen on a plastic tablecloth.

Oh, I had always had supper on the table—as soon as my husband got in from his job at Kennedy Space Center. The children knew what time to be there—never late because Daddy was to be honored with punctuality. But the idea of eating in the dining room was for company only.

After all, who had God given me who was more important than my family? No one. Absolutely no one!

Once I relaxed and settled into my own style, the family relaxed too and appreciated my special care.

WHAT IS A FAMILY?

Edith Schaeffer, a mother/author who knows, says:

A family is an economic unit—willing to live in conditions "better and worse" in different times of life, expecting to have ideas and a pioneering spirit of approach at times, but also having a deep understanding together that the family is not floating alone in an impersonal universe with no one to appeal to. We understand that God is there and that family members can, together as a unified group, come to him and say with honest belief and expectation, "Please God, do a new thing for us as a family, such as you speak of in Isaiah—make a way in the wilderness for us, and rivers in this desert" (see Is 43:19).[1]

HOMEMAKERS IN JESUS' DAY

Part of my changing outlook toward my family came when I read about the simplicity of hospitality in Jesus' childhood home. Finding out what Mary (the mother of Jesus) had to work with and the respect and love she earned, made me see it was not the candles that let my family know they are special.

A homemaker in Mary's time would begin her day at sunrise preparing a simple breakfast of curds and bread. Soon afterwards she might take her earthenware jug to the village well, letting the younger children go with her. Mary would wind her way down the narrow hilly streets toward the only well where cold pure water rushed from a fountain. After waiting her turn among the many other women, she would fill her jug, then move with extraordinary grace toward home, balancing the water jug on her stately head.

One or two days a week she walked down to the marketplace to shop at the farmers' crowded stalls and booths. Back home Mary would bake the day's bread supply—just one of her household duties. When weather permitted, she climbed to the rooftop of her small home to spin, weave, mend, wash, and make curds from goat's milk in a goatskin churn. The rooftop was also a good place to dry flax and clothes. On hot summer evenings the family liked to escape the oppressive heat of their tiny house by enjoying their evening meal in the open air on the rooftop.

During the rainy season, Mary would do her handwork inside her modest home—probably a one-room, square, dried mud brick building with whitewashed inside walls. Furnishings were sparse.

Before the evening meal the family washed their hands according to ritual. As they ate they used pieces of bread to scoop the food into their mouths. During the meal Joseph no doubt adhered to the scriptural admonition to teach his children God's ways. He would recite stories of their Hebrew ancestors, recalling God's commandments given to them through Moses. Just before Mary went to bed, she lit the fire in the oven and prepared the bedrolls for sleeping. Mary's daily routine varied little, except for Friday when she prepared the Sabbath meals in advance.

The Friday evening meal was a joyful occasion. Wives prepared special treats for their families in honor of the Lord. Families came to dinner dressed in freshly laundered tunics, ready for synagogue services afterwards.

TODAY'S HOMEMAKERS

Modern homemakers who believe they cannot have company for Sunday dinner because it would mean working on a day of rest, might look at Mary and her contemporaries. They had none of the modern kitchen conveniences we often take for granted. Today refrigeration helps! If you have a microwave you can warm up a dish quickly. So why shouldn't we follow this pattern of hospitality? Try it. You may be surprised at the blessing to your family and friends.

In fact, Laura fondly remembers the Sundays her whole family—three generations of them—gathered around the dinner table. One of her aunts regularly seated twenty-six at her table on weekends!

This was not just a time to eat because it was mealtime. It was a time for the family to share stories of the week and listen to each other. "My family heard the children as well as the adults," Laura reminisces. "There was a lot of laughter there too. I still remember some of the stories told and pranks pulled around the table when I was as young as eight or ten years old. We knew we were part of something special."

BACK TO THE NEST

But mealtime is not the only time we can make the family first in shared hospitality. In today's world, it is not uncommon for adult children to return to the nest for a season. Some come because of the slumping economy, some because they fit the pattern of the prodigal—and some simply because home is where their family is, where they feel they belong.

For the third time in her adult life, Shawn has moved in with her parents, Carolyn and Rob. At twenty-seven, it will be only a temporary stay—for financial reasons and to get to know her parents better, according to Shawn.

But for her parents, it has been a painful process having Shawn home. "We set some ground rules when she and her friend Barb came for three months. We would live as a family, and we would ask her to observe a two a.m. curfew. We also asked the girls to be here when we eat and to keep their rooms orderly. Both have rebelled about house rules."

The first time Shawn came home was in her sophomore year of college—pregnant by a married man. She had the baby, gave it up for adoption, then returned to earn her degree in sociology. The next time her younger brother came, too—both were independent young people who needed jobs and a place of security temporarily. It turned out they were frequently in agreement against their parents.

It was chaos. When Shawn broke curfew too many times, her parents asked her to move out. Her brother took up Shawn's offense, and he was almost expelled, too.

The third time Shawn took a job with the county probation

department and, though still at home, showed outright rebellion. Carolyn, a praying mom, felt God told her to "muster the troops" to pray that Shawn would not miss God's plan for her life.

Carolyn sees herself as many others of her generation—in their early fifties—as people stretched beyond elasticity. "We are an in-between generation, caretakers for our adult children and caretakers of our ill or aging parents. In addition to having Shawn home, we regularly visit Rob's mom in a nursing home and drive across the state to see about my own mom," she told me.

Communication and forgiveness are ingredients Carolyn considers paramount in having adult generations living with you. She has to ask Shawn's forgiveness quite a bit, because "A lot of my uglies come out when she reacts harshly or is unkind to me. I tell her she is valued, even when I don't approve of what she is doing—chasing men, smoking, wearing tight miniskirts—but I still love her and believe God will conform her to his image if she will only allow him to have control of her life."

Having children return to the nest can work. Bert and Charlene invited their married son, Lyn, and his wife, Julee, to live with them near Austin for the two years it will take them to save enough money for a down payment on a house of their own.

"This is a splendid arrangement for us," Bert told me. "We all four work, but Charlene and Julee take time for a Bible study together in the mornings. We enjoy our outdoor pool and generally catching up on the years we missed together while we were stationed in South America and Lyn was in the States in college."

Laura's son, Craig, left home and returned before he married at thirty-one and established a home of his own. Laura reminisces: "Those were good days, but sometimes hectic, too. Our small condominium was full of people when the three of us were home at once; our schedules were often disrupted by making way for one another. However, the blessings far outweighed the inconveniences. Craig still feels comfortable coming 'home' for a visit—in fact, it is one of my greatest joys to know that our children love to return to spend time with us—not all our friends can say that about their children, and it grieves me for what they are missing."

BENEFITS FROM TRAINING IN HOSPITALITY

A child will always reap lifelong benefits from training in family values. Five-year-old Marti loved to invite her playmate Barbara to share a lunch of "chicken 'oodle" soup. While their mothers caught up on neighborhood happenings, the little girls, at Marti's child-size table, served each other crackers and fruit— in training for grown-up hospitality.

In fact, Laura was sick when Craig had his eighth birthday. Twelve-year-old Marti said, "Kids need birthday parties. Mama, if you can bake his cake, I will do the rest."

It was St. Patrick's Day, so Marti thumbtacked green and white crepe paper streamers across the living room and dining room. She planned and directed games for the six little boys. She had as much fun as Craig and his friends.

Marti still enjoys family hospitality. Right now she is making plans for next Christmas. Along with Marti and Tom (and their five children—aged fourteen to twenty-two)—Laura and Brooks will be there. They hope to bring Laura's mother over from a nursing home on Christmas Day. Sometime during the holidays at least fifteen other family members will drop in.

Marti, who works outside the home, is still a good organizer. With everybody pitching in, preparing ahead, they expect to have a glorious time—from the Christmas Eve worship service to the last cookie crumb.

THE SANDWICH GENERATION

Psychologist Dennis Gibson, in *The Sandwich Years*, says:

Like butter between two slices of bread, we in our thirties through sixties find ourselves sandwiched between our children and our parents. Although our adult children need us less as parents and more as adult friends, our own parents are no longer able to care for themselves as they used to and increasingly need our help. Our nests have emptied, but we have new responsibilities toward the elderly members of our families.[2]

Laura and I both know what that means.

Not long after the Watsons moved into their new home, Laura's widowed mother needed special attention. Katherine, then eighty-one, could no longer live alone. Laura and Brooks brought her from Atlanta down to Florida so they could take her for medical diagnostic tests and plan for her future. They suspected Alzheimer's disease.

They put Brooks' home office furniture into storage, so they could move some of Katherine's furniture into the large room. They did everything they could to make her feel at home, even hanging her sheer blue curtains at the large windows that looked out onto a bed of bright zinnias Laura and Katherine planted.

For several months Katherine was content. But her personality changed completely.

One day we were sitting across from one another in the living room. I could tell Mother was trying to figure something out. Finally she looked up at me and asked, "Laura, who was your mother?"

I knew then that the doctors were on the right track. The neurologist confirmed our thoughts: Alzheimer's disease.

Mother was determined to go back to Atlanta—she took down her curtains and packed everything in sight. For two months she lived in that room with boxes in the middle of the floor.

Because she was still legally a Georgia resident, they could get financial assistance there. Marti—who lives in an Atlanta suburb

—said, "Mama, your own health is deteriorating rapidly. I will look around and find a good nursing home here where you want to be and where lots of our family live."

"Taking her to the nursing home was the worst day of my life," Laura remembers with a shudder.

At first she was very hostile, but after a year or so we were relieved that she felt happy and secure there. The personnel at the home shower her with love, and she now responds. She even sings softly much of the time.

Losing your memory is a terrible thing... but one of my sweetest blessings is to know that though Mother doesn't know what day it is, she remembers Scripture verses she memorized as a child. She truly did "hide them in her heart."

Brooks and I were so glad we had the ability to extend hospitality to Mother in her time of need. His office furniture is now back in place, and we use the room often. About all we can do for Mother at this time is to take care of her physical needs, visit her as often as we can, and pray. Always to pray.

Being the primary caregiver is a heartrending, and physically exhausting task. But what a privilege to be there for her when my mother was helpless, as she was there for me when I was a child and helpless. That is what family is all about.

MY OWN EXPERIENCE

I heartily agree. LeRoy and I moved into my mother's home to care for her when cancer became her enemy. She wanted to die at home, not in a nursing home or the hospital. The last three weeks were the worst.

Have you ever felt you reached the end of your endurance, when a stranger comes along to offer some cheery advice that cuts you to the quick? That is how I felt standing in the hospital's social services office late one afternoon.

The nurse assigned to help me check Mom out of the hospital told me pointedly, "I am sure your mom will say or do something so special you will always cherish the moment. You will be glad you took her home, regardless of the hardship of watching her suffer."

"But you don't understand," I protested, leaning against the door. "I have been taking care of Mom for a year now. I just can't take any more," I stammered.

She pushed a slip of paper into my hand. "Here is a list of nurses' aides who work in homes," she said warmly. "Try calling Harriet first. I will arrange for a registered nurse from the health agency to check your mom a couple of times a week."

As I turned to leave, she patted my knotted fist that clutched the crumpled list of names. I knew she meant well, but she could not possibly know how exhausted I was, nor how helpless I felt.

"Try Harriet first." Those words echoed in my ears. I dialed her number. Harriet, it turned out, was a remarkable woman who had thirty years of experience with nursing and death. Wearing a spiffy white uniform that set off her smooth chocolate brown skin, Harriet marched into our lives carrying a big leather bag that held her nursing apparatus and her embroidery work. The first day she proved to me she knew how to give sponge baths without hurting, how to turn Mom over with a sheet using the assistance of only one person, and how to coax her to take her medicine.

On the morning of my fiftieth birthday, Mom was in a semi-comatose state. I talked to her as though she understood, even though she could not respond. After repeating Psalm 23 and praying with her, I told her I would be right back and went to the kitchen for a cup of coffee.

I flipped on a recording of Mom's favorite choruses and hymns; I hummed along with the music. Just as I picked up my coffee cup I heard her yell something. "Why, she hasn't said a thing in days!" I reminded my sister, Ann, as we both dashed into Mom's room.

We watched as suddenly, through clenched teeth, Mom gave a weak shout. "Hallelujah! Hallelujah! Hallelujah!" That was all. A faint smile played across her face. But still she showed no sign of recognition of us.

Then I remembered what the social services nurse had said to me: She will say or do something so special you will always cherish the moment. You'll be glad you took her home.

Now I was glad—so glad—she had pushed me, even in my inward pain. For I might have missed that special moment to cherish when Mom gave me my best birthday present ever—her last words to me: "Hallelujah! Hallelujah! Hallelujah!"

OUR FAMILY STANDARD

We have had a special plaque hanging in our kitchen for years. It has blessed us and the many extended family members who have shared our home and our love.

> GOD MADE US A FAMILY.
> We need one another.
> We love one another.
> We forgive one another.
> We work together.
> We play together.
> We worship together.
> Together we use God's Word.
> Together we grow in Christ.
> Together we love all men.
> Together we serve our God.
> Together we hope for heaven.
> These are our hopes and ideals;
> Help us to attain them, O God;
> Through Jesus Christ our Lord, Amen.[3]

6

Extended Family

All who see them will acknowledge that they are a people the Lord has blessed.   Isaiah 61:9b

LEROY AND I HAD LIVED for almost thirty years in two locations in Florida. Now we were launching into a frightening new season of our life. Getting rid of most of our belongings and listing our house for sale, we loaded a truck with just enough furniture for a small two-bedroom apartment and headed for Dallas. LeRoy, now retired, would be a full-time student at Christ for the Nations Institute, where all three of our children had graduated. We would live on campus among students and faculty.

Soon after setting up housekeeping, we posted this plaque on our kitchen wall:

> Bless This Kitchen Lord
> And those who gather here each day.
> Let it be a place where we can meet
> To love and laugh and pray. Amen.

It was not long before a few "adopted" young people were gathering at our kitchen table to laugh and love and pray. One evening as we sat elbow-to-elbow with eight of them, I suddenly realized this was not too unlike my mom's boarding house in Tallahassee when I was in college. But this was more than feeding students. God was planting certain young people—mostly young men—in our extended family.

OUR CLAN

Greg had bounced into our lives before our son, Keith, graduated. We soon dubbed him "Number Two Son" because of the special place he held in our hearts. Not only did he eat with us often, but God kept me praying for the expansion of his God-given talents in music and preaching.

We prayed for Greg as he led the twelve hundred Christ for the Nations (CFNI) students in worship and when he went on mission trips to Spain, Nicaragua, and Germany using his musical gifts. His prayer life was more consistent than any young man I had ever met. I was blessed to know he prayed for me.

Even when he saw us almost daily, Greg sent us cards.

Dear Mama Quin and Papa LeRoy, I love you and appreciate all you've been and all you are to me, and I'll never take you for granted! Love, Your adopted son, Gregory.

After he graduated and moved from the men's dorm to his own one-room efficiency apartment, he phoned excitedly one day: "Mama Quin, I had my first dinner guest today—tablecloth and all!" My heart swelled with pride. He had learned well. Greg comes by often because he's truly a member of our family.

Other students have come and gone. David Carr, our "mercy son," helped with any task at hand—cooking, moving, helping LeRoy repair our cars and hauling our garbage downstairs to the dumpster every time he left our apartment. David had managed his dad's cotton plantation in Mississippi before attending Bible college. Today he serves the Lord in Argentina.

David Fowler, Aaron, and Bill joined Youth With a Mission's Mercy Ship—a floating hospital and evangelism boat—and sailed for Africa. Jerry B. took his new Irish wife, Marilyn, to Italy. Linda finally said yes to another Jerry after endless hours of talk with us. Debbie came for her prayer blessing before moving to Hong Kong to smuggle Bibles into Communist China.

Sharona, our Israel-born adopted daughter, is only twenty, yet she already has explored twenty countries. Still in Dallas working to complete her degree at another college, she comes to eat or spend the night with us almost every weekend, bringing laughter, love, and song into our lives.

Above my kitchen sink I keep a prayer board filled with pictures of all my "adopted" kids. Sharona made me a Hebrew sign to hang above it: *Mishpacha—Our Extended Family.*

Birthdays, graduations, and bon voyage provide times for celebrations with our young people. Prayer times in our apartment on Sunday nights are always exceptional. We pray about special requests of our extended family. One night Erin lacked $500 for her final school payment. Our kids gathered with us to pray. While we were still at it, several people called Erin's roommate, pledging a total of $520 toward Erin's bill. How we all rejoiced at the quick answer!

OUR FIRST EXPERIENCE

It seems a lifetime ago when LeRoy and I first experienced our "extended family." That Sunday morning Pastor Lord announced before his sermon, "Jesus, the Good Samaritan needs some innkeepers." A group of young people had come to work with our youth for a year, and they needed housing.

We already had invited one of those young men, twenty-three-year-old Mike, to come for Sunday dinner. Over dessert afterwards, we offered him our home if he was willing to share a room with our high-school-age son, Keith. A grin spread across his face. "Thanks, I will pray and let you know tomorrow."

As soon as he called to accept our invitation, I phoned our pastor's wife Johnnie for some advice, because they had been foster parents to several boys about Mike's age. She got right to the point with a list of guidelines:

- Make him part of the family immediately by giving him responsibilities—like making his bed and washing his own clothes. If you wait too long, it will seem like punishment, not a family responsibility.
- Plan things together as a family and be sure he knows he is included whether he can make it or not.
- Make time for him just as you would your own children. Let him know you love him just as he is.
- Correct him in love when necessary.
- Encourage him and pray for him in all his undertakings.
- Let him be free to bring his friends to your home, for it is now his home.
- Don't be surprised if the "honeymoon" is over in three months. Remember the real test of Christian commitment will come after this probationary period.
- He'll be a blessing to you, and God will honor your obedience to love and serve him through Mike.

WE ALL BENEFITED

Mike looked like a young Abe Lincoln with his dark beard and six-foot-three, slightly-bent frame. He would roughhouse with Keith, play the guitar for our morning family devotions, talk me into having sixty kids over for a youth party, and leave his smelly tennis shoes on the dining room table. Towels were left crumpled and toilet seats up after use.

But Mike was flexible, funny, and uncomplaining. He lived with us for more than a year. I prayed a lot for him—especially that God would give him a wife. Robin, a gifted schoolteacher, was the answer a year after he left us. Last Christmas they sent us a photo of their two youngsters with a note about their new church assignment in Ohio. I felt like a grandmother for the first time, since we have no natural grandchildren yet.

My enjoyable experience as a mom to Mike made my heart open years later to receive into our Dallas apartment those special young people God sent. I am so thankful LeRoy was willing to be Papa and allow me to be Mama Quin.

"This is all good," you say, "if you like that sort of lifestyle." But think about this: In our mobile society, God is putting the solitary into families. One way he does this is to form us into extended family groups. We often become closer to them than to our blood kin, loving them in the Spirit of God.

BACKGROUND OF THE BIBLICAL FAMILY CLAN

In Israel's early history, the Hebrew family was presided over by the oldest male, called "father" though he might, in fact, be a grandfather or great-grandfather. The extended family commonly included sons and their wives and children (Lv 18:6-18), and as many as four generations lived together. The extended family was part of a larger group called a clan. It might consist of hundreds of males (Ezr 8:1-14; Gn 46:8-27). They viewed each other as kinsmen and felt obligated to protect and help each other. Often the clan designated one man to extend help to clan members in need—he was called a *goel*, or kinsman-redeemer. Boaz, the next nearest of kin bought the field of the widow Naomi and married her daughter-in-law Ruth.[1]

But by New Testament times, it seems that the extended family was no longer as close-knit. Joseph and Mary, for instance, traveled as a couple to be taxed at Bethlehem and went alone when they took Jesus into Egypt. Scholars thus believe the New Testament family consisted of husband, wife, and children.[2]

Today when parents and children are isolated by distance, as God puts other young people into our lives, I am trusting he will have a family to engulf our own youngsters living in far-off parts. For instance, as I write this Quinett is spending the summer with Sharona's family in Israel.

In *Our Father Abraham*, Marvin Wilson shows that our Hebrew forefathers knew the importance of the home far more than we do today.

> After the destruction of the Temple in Jerusalem and the scattering of the Jewish nation into exile, the rabbis referred to the home as a small sanctuary or miniature temple. As a small sanctuary, the rabbis taught that the home, like the Temple, was to be set aside for special purposes. These included the worship of God (a "house of prayer"), the learning of Torah (a "house of study"), and the serving of the community needs (a "house of assembly")... Each home was to reflect God's glory through prayer and praise.[3]

The dinner table then became like an altar. Wilson goes on to discuss aspects of hospitality in the Jewish home:

> First, the rabbis considered hospitality as one of the most important functions of the home.... Second, one was not to discriminate in the showing of hospitality... the home was to be open to all classes and kinds of people.... Third, children were taught to be hospitable.... Fourth, guests were to be received graciously and cheerfully.... Finally, guests had a responsibility to the host... be grateful... offer a special

prayer for the host at the conclusion of a meal... not ruffle the host or cause him anxiety.[4]

LAURA'S LESSON

Laura was beginning to learn these lessons about the extended family at the same time I was, so many years ago. In fact, as prayer partners we were really in this thing together!

The buzzword in our circle was "minister to your families, creating wholesome relationships in the home." For Laura, this word from the Lord came with a real temptation to become ingrown. She tended to focus on her family only and forget to share God's love with a wide circle of friends and even strangers.

But Laura found there is room for everybody in the household of faith. Through contact with mutual friends, Loys Mundy stayed in the Watsons' home for a week. She was en route from Peru, where she was a secretary for Wycliffe Bible Translators, to Dallas, where she would receive further training for her job at Wycliffe's training center there.

Right away Loys fit into the household. "I don't recall ever being more blessed. Loys, we feel, is God's gift to us—I have always wanted a sister." Loys had no immediate family, only a few third cousins. During those thirteen long years she had been on the mission field in Peru, the church that sent her out had disbanded. All her close relatives had died. When she came home on furlough, there was no home to come to. All her roots had been pulled up.

Introducing her around the church, Laura got her eyes opened a little further. This same thing was happening all around. God truly was setting the solitary in families.

CAMPING IN THE KINGDOM

That taste of expanding family ties has continued to this day, with some delightful people being involved along the way.

Laura still likes to tell about one experience we had in our small home group:

Here we were at Boggy Creek, four families of us—and two dogs. My smile kind of drooped.

However, as I snuggled down into my warm sleeping bag I decided it wasn't so bad. In fact, it was great to be lulled to sleep by the antiphonal music of the whippoorwills.

Suddenly I was wide awake. Lonnie was gargling for a sore throat and the dogs had joined the chorus. Across the way in the Howards' tent, Linda had wrapped Frank's shirt around her head to keep her ears warm. Frank grabbed at her in the shadowy dimness and barked out, "What's this? What's this?" Linda's giggle rang out over the din. It was three a.m. Frank said, "I hear Wylene praying for the rapture."

The sun finally came up. LeRoy bounced out of his snug, virtually soundproof trailer intoning, "This is the day the Lord hath made." I could have killed him! Who wanted to get up this early after a sleepless night?

Brooks served everyone pancakes hot off the griddle. Quin fried a big pan of bacon. We worshiped the Lord while we toasted our toes around the campfire. As the day warmed up the kids scattered to pedal buggies and playground, the men left for the tennis court and swimming pool, and the women got out pencils and notebooks to share ideas for writing articles.

We were God's people, flowing together in his Spirit. His presence was real to us, and the false—if droopy—smile I had worn the previous day became real too. Even the dogs were at peace. We had a taste of living in the Kingdom of God on earth.

That is actually what an extended family life is all about—Kingdom living. It was a good start for my family. We eventually formed a camping group in our own church; it was not unusual for forty of us to go camping together. We took hymn books and Bibles and had worship services right there on the campgrounds. Sometimes other campers would join us.

Let Laura tell about another early experience:

"You're having chili?" our son, Craig, asked me. "Hmmm—think I'll fix some chicken and rice." Four young adults were milling around in our kitchen. I walked out on the confusion. None of them wanted the chili I fixed. I was glad I had an excuse to escape—Brooks and I had been invited out to dinner.

What had happened to my usually serene household? How could I learn to cope gracefully with these extra people? I had said before they came that if we are to live in extended families the rest of our lives, as our church was challenging us to do, I wanted to find out if I could take it for two weeks. Now here I was, copping out.

But the solution was quick in coming. Two Australian girls were staying with us while their group from the Redeemer Baptist Community (in Sydney, Australia) were in Florida. Leta, our 'adopted' daughter for some months, asked them, "How does your singing group blend their voices so well? Were you specially chosen or what?"

"Not at all," red-headed Carolyn answered with a smile. "There are some strong voices among us, and some weak, even two tone-deaf. We just listen to each other."

Blond Karen joined in. "Not just musically speaking, either. It is even more important that we be sensitive to each other and listen, so we can flow together all day every day."

They were living in the same neighborhood, in the same spiritual community, so they had to work together and play together. In harmony. The strong were not even tempted to take over, because there was discipline—the discipline of love.

Paul's words in Philippians 2:3-4 took on fresh meaning to

Laura: "Do nothing out of selfish ambition or vain conceit, but in humility consider others better than yourselves. Each of you should look not only to your own interests, but also to the interests of others." It was a good lesson in *harmonious* extended family life.

Yes, when you open your heart and your home to make people feel like family, you can expect some challenges. But if your heart is really open, you will experience multiplied blessings, too.

Christians can do without many things. But the one thing we all need is a family—a place to belong.

Loys lives in Dallas again, keeping house in a mobile home behind Wycliffe's training center, where she now works. But even though she is living in Dallas for the time being, the Tabernacle Church in Florida is still her home—"for when I come back and forth and perhaps some day sit kinda permanent-like." She has entered into the same kind of commitment as those who will never leave the Tabernacle.

Last summer Loys was at the Watsons' for several weeks. This time she more than proved her connection as a family member. Brooks had just had knee replacement surgery; Loys was there as an extra step-and-fetch-it person.

Just three months before Brooks' knee surgery, LeRoy had the same operation. It was our extended family—at least a dozen of them—who drove him clear across Dallas for physical therapy several days a week. We had a schedule worked out, and some would help with meals and errands. During his recuperation, while he was still on crutches, they would carry his books to class and run up and down stairs for him.

Loys belongs. Greg belongs. Mike belongs. All of our extended family members belong. What could be sweeter than, as my kitchen plaque says, our home being "a place where we can meet to love and laugh and pray."

7

Hospitality
and Tiny Tots

*We will tell the next generation the praiseworthy deeds
of the LORD, his power, and the wonders he has done.*

Psalm 78:4b

WHAT'S THE BEST WAY to handle entertaining when you have
tiny tots? There are several options:

1. Forget it.
2. Postpone it.
3. Include children the same age as yours.
4. Set an example.

Mary Ann, a twenty-nine-year-old mother of three preschool-
ers, gave up her career as a registered nurse to be a stay-at-home
mother. Setting up one room in her house as a playroom, she

often invites other mothers over with their small children so she can have adult conversation while they oversee their children.

She often invites couples with children for dinner. It is not unusual to have three couples, each having three children. Her husband Ralph sets up a picnic table in the dining room (with a sheet underneath to catch food spills) so the little ones can eat in the same room with the parents.

Mary Ann is sensitive to her children's needs and her husband's needs as well as her own. She has taught her youngsters there are certain times for different things: quiet time, Mommy time, Daddy time. Once a week Ralph takes one of the children (ages one, three, and five) with him for a ride or a meal out.

Barbie is a working wife and mother of a small boy. She loves to give parties—for any occasion. She keeps things simple, no matter what size group is invited.

"Usually we have just family, but those numbers add up, too, when you count the seven kids. Mark and the other men often gravitate to the den to play with his computer, and the young cousins can play in the backyard after dinner. We take lemonade to them out there while the adults have after-dinner coffee in the living room."

OTHER OPPORTUNITIES

Even with all these good ideas and opportunities, some families find that problems in certain situations dictate other solutions.

Laura decided feeding children separately was her best choice after one eventful evening some years ago. She had invited Brooks' distinguished boss and his socialite wife for dinner. Because they had no dining room, they all ate in the kitchen. Laura thoughtfully seated her guests so they faced the bright red poppy-printed curtains rather than looking toward the pans soaking in the sink.

The meal began smoothly enough. Then twenty-month-old

Marti stood up in her chair, pulled up her dress, patted her ball-shaped belly and asked one and all, "See my pot?" Marti then reached toward the butter, scooped up a bite and licked it off her finger, beaming at everyone at the table.

"That was the last time for several years that I tried to entertain at a meal with the kids present," Laura says. "After that they either ate early and went to bed before the guests arrived, or if our guests were bringing children of their own we fed them at another table in another room—out of sight and hearing if possible!"

Sensitive hosts may choose to invite just adults and make other arrangements for their own children's care while the party is in progress.

Our neighbors, who have a lively four-year-old, have company for dinner once a week. But they have discovered they do better if they get a sitter to entertain their little one and put her to bed. They look at their once-a-week "night out at home" as their Christian hospitality ministry as well as their own recreation.

Theresa, mother of two toddlers, has just dessert parties, timed so her children are already in bed when guests arrive.

Her most apparent problem is when friends pop in unexpectedly. She finally decided to quit apologizing for how her house looked. "I hope they come to see us, not our house anyway. I straighten the house in the morning, but if the girls get their rooms a bit disorderly during play, I have found I don't need to make excuses. Our house just has a 'lived in' look."

TRAIN UP A CHILD

Dr. Richard Dobbins, a Christian minister and licensed psychologist, says a child not only needs an example to follow, he needs instruction. "If there has been little or no instruction, the children will not know what is expected of them much of the time," he says.

"It's impossible to raise a child with no need for correction," he emphasizes.[1]

When Laura's daughter Kathy turned sixteen, Laura and Brooks gave her a plane trip to Dallas to visit Brooks' dad for a birthday present. On the big day, her granddad took Kathy and Dorie, a friend her age, to dinner at the country club.

Later Granddad reported to Laura and Brooks that he was very proud to introduce his friends to Kathy, pointing out that she was his granddaughter. "The contrast between Kathy and Dorie was striking. Good thing you take Kathy out to dinner often, so she knew how to behave. I was embarrassed by Dorie. Even though her dad is an executive at a big company in town, she had never been out to dinner before, and her folks just don't have company. It is going to be hard on her when she gets a little older."

Too often we forget children need to be exposed to good entertaining practices. How better can we teach our children manners and courtesy than by simply making it part of their home life? Dr. Dobbins points out: "Parents need to model for their children the way they want them to live. Children are great imitators. It is much easier for them to do what their parents say if they see their parents do it first."[2]

Four-year-old Lisa has watched her mother, Shirley, serve guests so often, that now she is allowed to be hostess at the children's table whenever company comes.

Children can be great helpers in home entertaining when we teach them the proper way to set a table, make a centerpiece or handle fragile dishes without dropping them. They gain self-confidence in their own social graces as they participate in our hospitality.

SEASONS OF HOSPITALITY

Discovering what works best for you will take a little experimenting. But we really do not have to forget about hospitality until the babies are grown. We just need to discover what our individual capabilities are for the moment and use them to our best advantage. There are seasons in our lives; in each we will find ourselves responding hospitably in a different manner. The time will come when your nest, like Laura's and mine, will be empty, the children far from home. Then there will be plenty of time left over for leisurely dining or more formal entertaining. And our children will stand up and bless us.

I believe our children grew socially as they were included in dinnertime conversation with our guests. Some of our friends have become their friends, too—sort of "adopted aunts and uncles." Quinett, Keith, and Sherry expanded spiritually, too, as we had missionaries, pastors, and even strangers dine at our table. One night Keith's eyes got very big while he listened, fascinated, to a young man who served a prison term, telling us how he accepted Jesus while behind bars. That story, told firsthand while it was still fresh, will be imprinted on our children's minds for a long time. I know, because they still talk about it years later.

JESUS CARES ABOUT CHILDREN

Children have a place in the heart of our Lord. Once when his disciples argued over who would be the greatest, Jesus stood a little child beside him and said, "Whoever welcomes this little child in my name welcomes me; and whoever welcomes me welcomes the one who sent me. For he who is least among you all—he is the greatest" (see Lk 9:47b-48).

Some years ago author Pat King wrote me about her own hospitality lessons. Mother of ten youngsters herself, she never knew when she would have an extra child to feed.

One morning I stopped in to see my friend Julie, who has four children under the age of five. Remembering my own days of little children, my heart often went out to her. As I let myself in the back door and heard the sounds of laughter coming from the children's bedroom, I peered in the doorway; there were Julie and her three oldest children sitting in a circle on the floor with a dishtowel spread out in the middle as a tablecloth. The baby watched from his bed as Julie poured water into the children's teacups and divided up the raisins and graham crackers. "Now Mrs. Jones," she asked her three-year-old, "would you like milk or sugar in your tea?"

Julie's smile acknowledged me in the doorway but she went on with her tea party as if she was entertaining the most important people in the world. I watched for a few moments, then slipped out the back door. Driving home, I thought about the women that day who would serve the Lord by entertaining those around them.

Says Linda Davis Zumbehl in her book *Homebodies:*

One day, when your children are grown and gone, you'll have time for a perfect house. What matters now is not the house, but the home; and not the children's duties, but the children. To every mother of young children who worries herself unnecessarily with trying to do too much, I can only say, "There is an appointed time for everything. And there is a time for every event under heaven" (Eccl 3:1 NASB).

If you're feeling overburdened by your responsibilities to church, school, and community, take heart. You can fulfill your duties as a good citizen when your kids are grown and in college. The most noble task you can do for God, and for your community, and for your country is to raise good citizens today. If that is all you accomplish in your lifetime, you will have accomplished more than most famous people![3]

Have you ever thought about the young boy who gave his lunch of two fish and five loaves of bread for Jesus to feed the crowd of more than five thousand people? I have. I can just imagine his mother packing it for him and sending him off with her blessings. Yet, hadn't she taught him hospitality, too? His small contribution was just what was needed that day for the meal to be remembered throughout history.

Prayer

Lord, help me to be hospitable when I still have little ones underfoot. Give me strength to extend my life to others—especially my children's friends. Help me to find a balance in this area of hospitality. May I be a hostess, Lord, whom my own children will do well to imitate. Amen.

8

Tradition Keepers

Only be careful, and watch yourselves closely so that you do not forget the things your eyes have seen or let them slip from your heart as long as you live. Teach them to your children and to their children after them.

Deuteronomy 4:9

"MOM, WHAT I MISS MOST are our family's spiritual traditions at Christmas," Keith said as we talked on the phone after his first Christmas away from home as a married man. "I just did not realize how much those family things mean to me—Christmas Eve services together, communion with the family, praying for one another."

"You will have to start your own traditions, Keith. Every family has something that means so much to them. When you have children, you will really want something special for them to remember."

"Yeah, I guess so..." his voice trailed off.

"Maybe you and Dana can continue the 'ten Boom New Year's Eve' tradition we have done for so long," I suggested.

CORRIE TEN BOOM'S TRADITION

When we moved to north Florida following LeRoy's retirement from NASA, we were part of a care group at Mike and Fran Ewing's home. A bonus was attending their New Year's Eve party each year. Because the Dutch evangelist Corrie ten Boom had used the Ewings' home as her "hiding place" for many years, her family's New Year's Eve tradition became theirs (and ours). Corrie's father, Caspar ten Boom, had celebrated this ritual all his life, and perhaps his own papa had before him.

Twenty to forty friends gather at the Ewing home for refreshments first. Then we took turns telling the highlight of what God did for us or through us that year that we wanted to thank him for.

Just before midnight Mike opened his Bible as Papa ten Boom had done, to read Psalm 90. When the clock struck midnight, we all hugged each other and cheered in the New Year. Always, from somewhere down the street, firecrackers exploded. The whole world had started a New Year.

More hugs, and we settled down for more Scripture reading. Just as the first words the ten Booms heard in the New Year were from Psalm 91, so were ours. Papa ten Boom read this favorite psalm to his family the last night they were together—the night they were taken prisoners by the Nazis for hiding Jews. Now Mike's strong voice spoke the familiar words: "He that dwelleth in the secret place of the most High shall abide under the shadow of the Almighty. I will say of the Lord, He is my refuge and my fortress: my God; in him will I trust..." (Ps 91:1-2 KJV). When Mike finished the entire psalm, Fran continued the Scripture Corrie always read: "Although the fig tree shall not blossom, neither shall fruit be in the vines; the labour of the olive shall fail, and the fields shall yield no meat; the flock shall be cut off from the fold, and there shall be no herd in the stalls: Yet I will rejoice in the LORD, I will joy in the God of my salvation" (Hb 3:17-18 KJV).

Then Fran repeated Corrie's usual admonition: "Don't forget, no matter what happens in the life of a child of God, the best remains. The best is yet to be."

Next, some of the men served communion—cups of grape juice and morsels of bread. I don't know if this part was done in the ten Boom household, but it is at the Ewing's house. Many families through the years from the Ewing care group have continued this New Year's Eve custom, no matter to what corners of the world they moved. Now Keith, too, could celebrate it with his new wife at midnight on New Year's Eve.

Traditions. We either love them or fear them. But we all have them.

Any custom that has been repeated must have started with a good idea. The problem comes when we forget why we still dutifully perform the function.

Mabel says she gives gifts at Christmas—or at any other time—to remember and honor Jesus, God's perfect gift to us. That is a good reason to continue.

So let's consider how we can build *God-honoring* traditions to make ours a household of blessing.

BIBLICAL TRADITIONS

Jesus often broke bread with his disciples at the close of the day, using the occasion to teach them important things about God. As far back as Old Testament times the Israelites were fervent tradition-keepers, enjoying their celebrations, feasts, or festivals—holy days. Even today they break out into singing and dancing at the slightest excuse to celebrate. I have seen Israelis on the streets of Jerusalem, arms locked, dancing for no apparent reason but for happiness.

After Quinett had lived in Israel almost a year, she suggested our family start celebrating Passover—with a Messianic emphasis. We saw the beautiful symbolism in how our Lord chose Passover as his last meal with his friends, and how it spoke to them about his body and blood he was about to give in death for them. The Passover Lamb himself was about to be sacrificed.

Returning to the Jewish roots of our Christian faith, we make preparations for this feast. We mix chopped apples, honey and nuts for *kharoset;* we buy *matzah* (unleavened bread), *maror* (bitter herbs), horseradish, parsley, a leg of lamb....

On Passover night, with fresh candles in place in our menorah, eight to twelve of our extended family come to the table in their Sunday best. We light the festive candles, observe the handwashing ceremony to start the ritual, then enjoy the two-hour meal and service around the table. As our Passover seder comes to a close, Greg, our musician, sings Psalm 136, pausing at the end of each verse so we can all say, "His love endures forever."

Haggadah means "the telling." The story of Passover has been told and retold for thousands of years, a story from slavery to freedom. The original Passover commemorated God's deliverance from Pharaoh's tyranny, as the Israelites put the blood of an unblemished lamb on their doorposts so the death angel would pass over their houses.

When we commemorate Passover, we thank God for Jesus Christ, our slain Passover Lamb who made atonement for us, freeing us from the bondage of our sins.

Many who have heard about our Passover celebration have asked how they could get a "pattern" for doing a Passover meal in a Christian home.

We wrote our own outline at first. But recently someone gave us a small booklet written especially for Christian families to use, *The Messianic Passover Haggadah.* (For their address, see the list of recommended books in the appendix.) Explanations and Scriptures are in Hebrew and English. The Lederer Foundation also publishes booklets to help celebrate the Feast of Trumpets, Feast of Tabernacles, Festival of Dedication, and a Messianic children's curriculum for the various feasts.

Says Vivian Hall in *Be My Guest:*

> All special days are not directly connected to our spiritual heritage, but all celebrations within a Christian home should reflect a spiritual emphasis. Romans 14:6 tells us that he who regards one day as special does so to the Lord. Our celebrations need to be God-honoring.[1]

Traditions help preserve the memories. Besides Deuteronomy 4 at the beginning of this chapter, we have a biblical injunction in the Psalms admonishing us to keep alive God's mighty deeds from generation to generation: "I will open my mouth in parables, I will utter hidden things, things hidden from of old—things we have heard and known, what our fathers have told us. We will not hide them from their children; we will tell the next generation the praiseworthy deeds of the LORD, his power, and the wonders he has done" (Ps 78:2-4).

With the wonders of camcorders and tape recorders, it is much easier to keep family memories alive today. Before my mom died, she retold into a tape recorder her favorite family stories from her childhood and from the perspective of a single mother rearing four children.

Keeping a memory book or tapes are good ways for one generation to pass on to another their legacy. I have kept a prayer journal for over eighteen years. Anyone who reads it after I am gone will certainly see the faithfulness of God in the way he answered so many prayers.

EASTER

From establishing an Easter tradition, Laura found a good opportunity to build memories with her grandsons.

Since spring break often coincides with Easter, it is a time when teenagers Troy or Chris often visit. They might spend a whole morning dyeing eggs decorating them imaginatively—Chris, in particular, has a lot of artistic talent.

"Last year," Laura says, a twinkle in her eyes, "I thought they were getting a little old for this. But Marti—Troy's mom—noted that the boys might say they were humoring Gran-'ma'am, but in reality they really wanted an excuse to stay little kids a while longer."

One year Laura and Chris had just finished cleaning up the messy kitchen and were getting a bit slap-happy. Irene, Chris' mom, came in and asked, "Shall we hide the eggs now?"

Chris' eyes lit up. "Sure!"

About the time Irene and Laura had pushed the last egg under a sofa cushion, Laura's son Craig came in. "Mom! Irene! What are you doing? Can I help Chris find them?" Then Brooks came in… so all the guys, from granddad to son to grandson, hunted Easter eggs.

Not a very "spiritual" way to celebrate Easter, you might say. But making family memories across the generations is a very spiritual thing to do, Laura believes. "We dye eggs as a 'together' project, not involving the Easter bunny but celebrating the newness of life that Jesus gave us."

MOTHER'S DAY

With our "family" now including so many young folk far from their homes, Mother's Day becomes a great time to celebrate our heritages. LeRoy and I prepare a real feast for Mother's Day. Then we ask all those seated around our table to recall a special contribution his or her mother has made in their lives.

Many times, because they are mostly young folks missing Mom, I will see teary eyes as they tell about what their mothers have meant to them, especially if that mother has blessed her child in Jesus' name.

BIRTHDAYS

Birthdays, too, are natural occasions for honoring the Lord while honoring one another.

Harry and Elizabeth Stuart are parents of five adult children. They all get together only twice a year. But they save those special times to celebrate everyone's birthday—once at the Carolina resort where they go in the summer, then again at their Lexington home at Thanksgiving or Christmas.

We take presents for everyone in the family who has had a birthday from January through July and have a big party at the beach hotel for all of them—our children, their spouses, and even the grandchildren.

Then we do the same for family members whose birthdays come in the last half of the year. Depending on which holiday most of them can come to our home, we celebrate this time either at Thanksgiving or Christmas, Elizabeth explains.

"Birthdays are special, personal times for us. We want to remember them together."

Ruthanne's husband John came up with a novel way to remember her birthday. He asks all her friends to phone her the morning of her birthday to extend best wishes. She is inundated with calls!

FOURTH OF JULY

Every July 4, Dottie's family has a reunion in their Florida hometown. This year they will gather at her brother's new cottage behind the original homestead.

"Buddy's house is small, but the yard is enormous. There will be plenty of room for the thirty to thirty-five of us to spread our covered dish picnic on tables under the big live oaks. We will sit around and tease each other and tell and retell family stories. It is a good way to keep up with everybody all at once, and to keep up the family continuity for the younger generation."

THANKSGIVING

We don't have to wait for the specified dates of holidays to celebrate. I once threw a Thanksgiving feast in August. I had learned that Beth and Floyd Alves, whom our Ewing care group helped to sponsor on the mission field, were in the area. I called the families and invited them to our house on Friday night: "Beth and Floyd are always in Europe and miss out on an American Thanksgiving. I want to surprise them. Could you bring the vegetables to go with my turkey and cornbread dressing?"

That weekend, as seventeen of us gathered to remember our forefathers' traditions with thanksgiving, we had communion together, sang "God Bless America," and wept a bit over God's linking us all together. It was a Thanksgiving I will never forget.

CHRISTMAS

Elizabeth Mizell and her son-in-law Ralph have a tradition of Christmas shopping together every year. Somewhere around the first of December they will set out for Orlando—fifty miles away—very early on Saturday, eating breakfast in the mall before shopping for the next eight hours. They will eat lunch together but get home in time for dinner.

"It is our day together," Ralph told me. "And I wouldn't miss it for the world. My mother-in-law is a fun person. She has some great ideas for gifts for my wife as well as surprises for our three children."

Elizabeth grinned. "No mother-in-law jokes for us! We are family."

Carmen, mother of six adult children, says they have to draw names for gift-giving now that her children have children of their own.

"We get one nice present for the person whose name we draw. But all through December we surprise that person with small gifts. We are never allowed to tell who the gift-giver is. Makes it more fun, keeps us guessing," she said with a soft laugh.

I can look around my house even now and see gifts friends made for me one Christmas when our pastor challenged us to use creativity in our gifts: a stained glass angel, a poster framed with cedar, a cross-stitched Bible verse, a Christmas card of Mary and Jesus decoupaged on a plaque...

For Christmas each year I write a letter to each of my children, an epistle of encouragement. I have been doing this for over twenty years; if I am late they let me know about it!

During Christmas holidays when her grandchildren all visited her, Mary Jo ushered them into her van and drove to homes of her special friends, so the youngsters could hop out and sing Christmas carols while Grandma Mary Jo left the family some of her baked goodies. While we lived in the same town, I always looked forward to being one of those "special friends."

WEDDINGS

Wedding customs are changing, with more and more brides and grooms writing their own vows, picking a theme that is carried out in music and Scriptures, making their wedding reflect their personal relationship with Jesus Christ.

My son Keith and Dana had chosen "Covenant Celebration"

as their wedding theme. Everything in it pointed to covenant, a solemn agreement between God and man, from the pastor's message to the program they gave to all the guests.

A processional of worship banners, including one specially designed and hand-made by Keith's sister Quinett, began the ceremony, with music from Steve Fry's "Unto the Lord." Other personal touches they used were:

- the blowing of a ram's horn, the shofar
- a time to publicly thank their parents, but to announce they were leaving and cleaving to one another
- laying on of hands for prophecy and prayer by specially invited ordained ministers (the groom is in missions)
- the recessional with the congregation singing "Crown Him with Many Crowns."

One of our family wedding traditions has the bride and groom returning to one of their homes after the wedding reception to watch a video of the event, to open presents and to have a "last meal" with both sides of the family. This helps in bonding the two families, making memories for all.

After Keith and Dana's wedding reception, we served a simple meal to almost forty family members who crowded into our small Dallas apartment. Some aunts and uncles had come from so far away, they appreciated this opportunity to see and talk with the newlyweds. Since the bride and groom were spending the night in town, it was their idea to do what their cousins before them had done—spend time with the family before leaving on their honeymoon in Hawaii.

FUNERALS

Traditions for funerals are changing, too. There is a growing trend to bury the dead with only the family present at the graveside, then to go to the church for a memorial service. Here several people might give a eulogy or testimony. Following that, sometimes some members of the church provide a meal for the family in the church fellowship hall, keeping the nursery open for the youngsters.

This was done for my brother-in-law's funeral. Some church members do the clean-up as well, saving the family from work.

When Jamie Buckingham died, the burial was private, with only family and a few close friends present. Then the home group (he and Jackie had been members for fourteen years) served a meal at the home for the family. A week later a large memorial service was held in the church he pastored. Again the home group hosted a reception, for several hundred out-of-town guests so they could greet Jackie.

TRADITIONS THAT MAKE OTHERS FEEL LIKE FAMILY

I have kept a guest book for many years. One time I was surprised to count over one hundred and forty people who had come to our home within a two-month period. As I pored over the pages, I was delighted to reminisce about those occasions. One of my friends told me that knowing a record of his visit is important to me made him feel more like part of our family.

Another remembrance record we keep is our big "Welcome Home" sign we take to the airport whenever we greet our extended family members—most of them Bible school students or graduates—returning from overseas. They write on the back of the sign their name, date, and country from which they are returning. Then I snap their photo for our album.

In the past eighteen months, they have signed after coming from Israel, Italy, Ireland, Spain, Germany, Africa, Singapore, Malaysia, Argentina, England, Denmark, and Holland. They all look for THE SIGN because one of us will be there to greet them with it. We have some of the neatest pictures—from weary travelers to young people sporting silly grins and wearing various kinds of hats they have bought in the country where they had gone to minister.

Every time the Watsons have overnight guests, Brooks makes pancakes for breakfast. This skill was developed when their children were small. "We never would have made it to church on time if Brooks hadn't done K.P. on Sundays," Laura says.

Now this has become such a tradition that last Christmas Marti gave her dad an apron, a chef's hat, and a potholder set.

Laura is in a regular Thursday-at-three tea-sippers group. They first got together when one of them (Linda) invited a couple of her friends to share her afternoon tea break. Linda accompanied her husband on a business trip to England where this custom caught her imagination. The news spread, and the three or four of them became nine or ten.

These friends all stay pretty busy during the week. Several have outside jobs and all of them are active in the work of the church. But they set aside an afternoon each week to relax at the tea table. They alternate homes, and each woman has her own unique style for setting a pretty table.

How in the world could they justify taking two hours out of the heart of the week just to drink tea, swap magazines and catalogs, and talk about recipes and roses and "tea bags are good to lay on puffy eyes"?

Well, aside from "a merry heart doeth good like a medicine" (Prv 17:22 KJV), "… the joy of the Lord is your strength" (Neh 8:10). We do usually take ourselves too seriously. But not this bunch! They have joy!

Their blessing often includes thanking God for the fun they have defusing tension and stress. However, not only do they laugh together—when one of them is hurting, they pray together, too. They have discovered that is what real fellowship is all about. As God draws them closer together, he draws them closer to himself as well. They truly are strengthened by joy in him.

Do you need a "family" to share your heart with? Invite someone to tea.

THE BEST FAMILY TRADITION: PRAYER

Recently Laura came across a letter her Uncle Ted, a missionary, had written to his mother on her eighty-first birthday:

> *Mother, the dearest memory I have of you is when one day I ran into the house to get a baseball bat, and as I opened the door I saw you there on your knees, praying for your children. Your prayers have certainly followed your children. Every one of us thanks God for such a wonderful, God-fearing, praying and loving mother.*
>
> *Thank God that our every memory of you is one of beauty and holy living and rare parental guidance. Every one of us will be able to remember our family prayers morning and night. And how you taught us the Scriptures...*

Laura's grandmother went to heaven just three months after receiving that letter. But her prayers and the influence of her godly life are still an *active* blessing for her children, grandchildren, great-grandchildren, and a fast-growing number of great-great-grandchildren. Following a family reunion several years ago, Laura realized that all her grandmother's descendants were Christians. What a responsibility that put on her to pray regularly, as her beloved grandmother had, for her own grandchildren. But what a privilege!

What a heritage to ponder. What a tradition for all mothers (and all of us) to follow: pray for our children (and others in our extended family), pray *with* our children (and others), and live a godly life before them. The results are always far-reaching. Heaven will be full of the evidence.

PART THREE

Blessings of Special Friends

9

Open House Blessings

Is not this the kind of fasting I have chosen: to loose the chains of injustice and untie the cords of the yoke, to set the oppressed free and break every yoke? Is it not to share your food with the hungry and to provide the poor wanderer with shelter—when you see the naked, to clothe him, and not to turn away from your own flesh and blood? Isaiah 58:6-7

IN LUKE 22 IS A PASSAGE about preparation for the Passover. Have you ever wondered about the people who made these preparations?

It was the custom of the inhabitants of Jerusalem to receive Passover celebrants as brothers. They furnished space in rooms or apartments where travelers might eat the feast. So the disciples asked Jesus if there were a particular house where he wanted them to prepare the Passover meal. Jesus told them they would see a man who carried a pitcher of water: follow him to the chosen house.

It makes me wonder about the others involved, those in the background. To begin with, it was unusual to see a man carrying water—that was women's work. Did the man with the pitcher know someone would be looking for him? Not likely. Did the householder know who would be celebrating, using his house? No. But Jesus knew, and he knew how to find the right place.

What a blessing, to be of service to him like this, and for what a purpose: his last meal with his disciples. There was no way for the householder to have known the importance of what was to take place that night. I wonder if he ever did know while he was on this earth. But open house hospitality was a way of life for him. He was ready for whoever came. Here is an example showing hospitality is not just for women.

MISFIT GUESTS

Are you ready for whoever comes? What about guests who don't fit in?

For instance, there was a young woman (Pat) who several times came to our dinner table and saw the candles already lit. "LeRoy, switch on the lights overhead. I don't like candlelight," she demanded. LeRoy would always do it to please her.

When I asked a friend how to handle this, she suggested that I lovingly but firmly say, "Pat, we like candlelight. You are our guest; we are not yours. When we are on your turf, you are in charge."

However, I wonder.... Our friend Jamie would have said, "It is better to be kind than to be right" and, like LeRoy, turn on the lights. There are no hard and fast rules about some situations. Surely Pat did not mean to be offensive—she was just unthinking and probably unschooled in good manners. But do remember when you are a guest—be careful to fit into your hosts' plans.

Am I so in tune with Jesus that he could send someone to me? Am I prepared to serve him? Am I willing to remain in the background—to cook food and wash the dishes, to watch the baby while my guests spend the day at the beach, to make beds, to lend my car—or my time?

We need to ask ourselves these hard questions if we determine to follow Jesus' call to service. He said if we serve even the least of our brothers, we are serving him whether or not we realize it. If I would be ready to serve him at all times, hospitality must become a way of life for me.

It really is not that hard when we have God's guidance.

When Laura and Brooks were planning to build their house, they were convinced God wanted them to use their new house to bless many people. Laura explains:

We designed one long room for the living/dining room. That way, when we have a big crowd for a meeting, we can push the furniture into the dining area where we have a drop-leaf table. When we have a big crowd for a meal, we can shove sofa and chairs back and add leaves to the table. I usually serve a crowd buffet style; with everything in one big room, it is convenient as well as comfortable.

Whenever we express hospitality through our homes, we can be sure we are on safe scriptural ground. Even a casual reading of the Old Testament impresses us with the way those folks showered hospitality on friends and strangers through their homes. Gracious hosts not only fed and provided overnight lodging for guests—as they did Jesus and the disciples for the Passover—but they often cared for the servants and animals of their guests as well.

In the New Testament we also read about believers enjoying food and fellowship with each other, "... breaking bread from house to house,... taking their meals together *with gladness and sincerity of heart*" (Acts 2:46 NASB, italics mine). Whether it was a simple meal or a feast, whenever God's people got together, they worshiped the Lord and enjoyed fellowship with one another.

One Sunday night our church members celebrated our own feast following a day of fasting. Calling it "A Feast of Homes," some fifteen hundred of us gathered in sixty-four different homes in family units to enjoy a meal, worship, and the Lord's Supper.

Thirty-four people brought food to our house. After we enjoyed a leisurely meal, we moved to the living room where our leader read from the Bible and led us in communion. Some children, sitting on the floor, began to sing as we broke the loaf of home-baked bread, symbolizing the broken body of Christ.

I closed my eyes to concentrate on the joyful songs of praise, piped in children's voices. My heart was touched. This could have been a New Testament church commemorating the death of Christ—right here in our home.

As the cup of juice was passed, I wondered if it had been like this after the Day of Pentecost when those new Christians were "continually devoting themselves to the apostles' *teaching* and to *fellowship*, to the *breaking of bread* and to *prayer*" (Acts 2:42 NASB, italics mine).

I closed my eyes once more, this time trying to imagine what it was like when Jesus visited the home of Lazarus, Martha, and Mary. There he always received a hearty welcome. I have the idea he felt free to drop by any time.

I wondered how Jesus first met this family. Was he walking one day down the dusty road through Bethany when Martha came out, offered him a cup of cold water, and invited him in to share their evening meal? Or were they perhaps among the first crowds who sat on the hillsides listening to his parables?

Martha's generous ministry must have revolved around food. She was a careful and considerate hostess, concerned about details.

KILL A CHICKEN?

How should we then live? Certainly not like my mother's elderly aunt.

When Mama was a little girl, she and her parents were invited to visit an aunt who lived some miles from them. It was agreed they'd arrive on a certain day before suppertime. They had to leave home before one a.m. to get there by early afternoon. The four kids were hungry as could be. But no food was offered. Suppertime approached, and the children were fidgity, cranky, and hungry! Finally old Aunt Bessie pushed herself out of her wicker rocker on the front porch and headed toward the back-yard.

"Well, I guess I had better go kill a chicken," she announced to her six starving guests.

Go kill a chicken? Not only had she not started supper, she had not even killed the chicken intended for their evening meal. No wonder my mama grew up wanting to feed people properly!

Being prepared ahead of time for company saves a lot of hassle. Fortunately most of us don't have to kill the chicken we are to serve. But we do all have to learn how to be hospitable, which is why I have tried to teach my children by example.

HOW MANY, MOM?

Sherry was a teenager when she got her own personalized lesson. "How many coming for dinner today?" she asked when we got home from church.

"You can set four extra plates. Daddy invited some visitors to come eat with us."

"Why, Mom?" she complained as she jerked open the silverware drawer. "Why do we *always* have company on Sunday?"

"Well, it is one way we can share Jesus' love. Those people drove a long way to attend our church. Daddy wanted to bring them home to eat so he could have more time to talk with them about the Lord."

Handing her the dinner plates, I shuddered a moment, remembering all those years I wasted. All those years I neglected to invite others into our home, even LeRoy's friends from work. I had some real hang-ups. I thought I had to be a gourmet cook—as well as live in a decent-sized house—and be a witty conversationalist before I would be comfortable inviting company for dinner.

Then, new in town, I stumbled on a way to be hospitable, the day Lib and Gene invited us home for lunch. It was a start. But I really got liberated the day I read something from Paul in the Living Bible: "... you should practice tenderhearted mercy and kindness to others. Don't worry about making a good impression on them..." (Col 3:12b).

What freedom that gave me. I could just relax and be myself. I was finally realizing all Jesus requires of me is to be available to share his love with others.

HINTS THAT BLESS

Over the years I began to talk with mature Christian women who were willing to share their hospitality hints with me. Some of them I could adapt for our home. Others were not practical for us.

The following are a few they shared with me, as well as a few of my own.

Prayer. We saturate our home with prayer *before* our invited guests arrive. Usually my husband and I pray together, asking God to express his love through us. We also pray that our guests will feel the presence and the peace of the Lord in our home.

Music. We play Christian music *softly* on the stereo as guests arrive, helping create an atmosphere of praise.

Greeting. When people come to our home for the first time, we welcome them in the name of the Lord Jesus. When I introduce people, I try to find a mutual point of contact so they can start talking. I will say something like, "You have something in common. Both of you are excellent seamstresses." Or, "Joe just moved here from Miami. I know you used to live there, too, Malcolm."

I try to have a listening heart and seek out guests who are lonely and get them to talk. Jesus told us to be careful how we listen.

Blessing. If we have too large a crowd to sit at the dining table, we gather in the living room, stand in a circle and hold hands while LeRoy offers the thanksgiving prayer. When we entertain business associates, even if they are not Christians, we always say the blessing before the meal. After all, the Lord is our provider and we want to thank him.

Co-host. When we are having a large group of people over, I like to ask a friend to assist. We can swap working in the kitchen.

Not wasteful. While we prepare the meal, we pray, asking God to make it nourishing and attractive. Sometimes we have to pray he will show us how to stretch it to feed a few extras. We try not to be wasteful. After Jesus fed the five thousand, he had the disciples gather up the fragments. So I learned to save leftovers to use in soups, salads, or casseroles. Rather than throwing out coffee—freeze it, or iced tea—save it for punch, or even leftover bread—make it into crumbs for casseroles.

Prepare in advance. Preparation ahead of time is vital. During the six years we were in Pastor Peter Lord's church where company every Sunday was routine, it meant preparation time was spent every Saturday. Then on Sunday, with table already set and food only needing to be rewarmed, we could sit down to a meal without a lot of fanfare in the kitchen.

I also learned to keep extras in the pantry for unexpected guests—cans of beans to add to a pot of chili, tuna to add to boiled eggs and relish for a quick lunch, extra bread in the freezer, packages of instant pudding, lots of rice and potatoes.

Remember Mama's old aunt who had not killed the chicken for supper? While we don't go out and kill a chicken these days, I have learned many creative ways to prepare dishes with one boiled, deboned chicken—from a Chinese chow mein dish to a Mexican tortilla chip concoction. And I am sure you too can feed up to twenty on one chicken, if you use some creativity.

Keep records. Keep an indexed file of favorite recipes, sorted according to beverages, desserts, meat dishes, salads, and vegetables. I also try to keep a record of what I served to whom and when so I can vary the menu when I have some of the guests back again.

Hot drinks. In winter I no longer serve fresh perked coffee. Instead, I fill the thirty-six-cup coffee maker with water and plug it in. Guests are invited to make their own hot drinks using the instant mixes I set out—herb teas, cocoa, mocha, or coffee. I have much less waste now.

Wives, let hubby help. My husband is a marvelous host at the door, greeting guests and making them feel truly welcome. When our house buzzes with guests who come for a late supper, he is in the kitchen helping refill an empty punch bowl while I replace sandwiches. Or he is off in a corner talking to a bashful soul who is lost around lively talkers. Hospitality is not something the wife does on her own. Whether the wives are staying at home or working outside the home, husbands can be involved in helping to prepare the home for guests, and then in serving the guests.

Don't apologize. Never apologize for how the house looks if company comes in unexpectedly. I try to keep our house "picked up" so it looks orderly. But if it isn't spotlessly clean, I do not want to draw attention by saying, "Oh, my house is a mess. I have not cleaned the bathrooms yet."

Try to remember guests have come to see you, not your house; you want to be gracious to all your guests—especially those who pay you the honor of dropping in unannounced.

Children practice too. When our children were teenagers, we let them invite their friends for Sunday dinner. They liked to offer the invitation, help cook the meal, then assist in serving. Afterward we all sat in the living room and visited. It helped us get to know our children's friends better and gave our youngsters a chance to practice hospitality.

Strangers for meals. We often invite college kids home after church for a meal. It meant so much to our own college youngsters far from home when a family invited them after church for a home-cooked meal. So we can reciprocate by doing the same for lonely youth here.

Great heritage. One of the greatest heritages we can give our children is to have them share our table with great men and women of God. This does not mean we invite all the guest pastors or missionaries home to eat after they speak at our church. But we do ask the little widow who depends on God for every need, the lonely schoolteacher who's spent her life joyfully caring for her aged mother, or the retiree who's served God in the factory where he has worked all his life.

IDEAS FOR PARTIES

The various types of parties mentioned here are familiar in our area. Some of them may be adaptable to your situation.

Brown bag lunch. Sometimes called "poor boy" suppers, these are increasing in popularity, especially among younger people.

Everyone brings a sack lunch. Guests sit out under the trees eating picnic style. In case of rain, they move into the living room and sit on the floor, listening to stereo music. The host usually furnishes the beverage.

Spur of the moment. Don't hesitate to ask another family to bring their Sunday dinner and combine it with yours. Some of the greatest fellowships have been dinners when two or more families combined their meals at a home, a park, or at the beach. Look what this did for me!

Cook out. Laura's son, Craig, often cooks supper on his back porch grill. His wife, Irene, works, so it is a big help that he likes to do this. In fact, all the Watsons' kids like to grill their supper, especially when company is coming. So last Christmas Laura and Brooks gave each of them an electric *indoor* grill—no need to wait for summer for those succulent chops and hamburgers. Plus, when there is a crowd, using both indoor and outdoor grills speeds up meal preparation.

Glory party. These sessions are sometimes also called "prayer and praise" parties because they are held to praise the Lord. They include much singing, from old-time favorites to Scripture choruses. A guitarist is an asset. If you have rhythm band instruments such as tambourines, triangles, maracas, or cymbals, let each guest choose which one to play to "make a joyful noise unto the Lord." Serve light refreshments after a time of singing and prayer so guests will have an opportunity to visit over the punch bowl.

Count it all joy. When you are experiencing trials, throw a "joy party." This is a time when you least feel like celebrating anything. But James 1:2 tells us to "count it all joy" when we go through testings. Invite some of your closest friends over for a backyard picnic. You will be surprised how you will be lifted up after these Christians have prayed for you and shared your burden.

Dessert party. Invite friends over *after supper* for dessert. You can furnish the food or ask the guests to bring their favorite homebaked goodies, perhaps with the recipe to share. Or ask everyone to bring fresh fruit. This is a good mixer party for newcomers or to get acquainted with the neighbors. After eating, you can visit, sing some songs, or play charades.

In the intervening years since I started seating our family in the dining room amid candlelight, a host of others have joined our buffet suppers. It has not been unusual to have anywhere from forty-five to sixty people in our home each week—some for prayer meetings, others for meals, still others just to talk and snack.

Jesus is setting me free to be more flexible in some of my attitudes. Now when an invited guest asks, "What can I bring?" I am likely to say, "What would you like to bring?" I have found most people have a favorite dish they like to cook; if they ask, they are serious in their offer to bring some food. So I let them.

I have also found that it is the Christian fellowship that draws people, not the scrumptious food. If we are truly facing hard times of shortages, we need to have this attitude firmly in place. I heard Jamie Buckingham say, "We have got to learn to love and serve others during prosperous times, so in hard times it will come naturally."

When you are acting in God's will, the blessings of open house hospitality come upon you in showers too wonderful to measure. And you begin to see that loving others is what hospitality is all about anyway—we need each other.[1]

10

The Prophet's Chamber

Let's make a small room on the roof and put in it a bed and a table, a chair and a lamp for him. Then he can stay there whenever he comes to us. **2 Kings 4:10**

"HONEY, TAKE MY BIBLE up to the bedroom for me, will you please?" LeRoy called to me. He was rushing out the front door to catch his ride to work.

After I grabbed the laundry basket, I found his Bible on the kitchen table, tucked it under my arm and started upstairs. Yesterday he left his Bible on the back porch chair. Why is his Bible always in a different spot? I asked myself.

Surprised, I realized my husband had no place in our house to call his own.

For his morning devotions he shifted from living room to den, from back porch to kitchen. Clanging pots, pans and dishes made his "quiet time" anything but quiet. He simply had no privacy.

As I folded the towels, I remembered a conversation I had with our pastor after church one recent Sunday.

"You said in your sermon that the husband is the prophet and priest of the home. Will you explain that more thoroughly?" I asked.

He rubbed his hands together and smiled.

Look at it this way. God says in his Word that the husband is the head of the home. As your husband goes to God on behalf of the family, he is acting as *priest*—standing before God. Of course, as believers we are all "priests" but we are talking about the husband as the head of the home. When he hears from God for the family, he is *prophet*, passing down God's direction to the family. That's what I meant about his role as prophet and priest.

For several days I had mulled over his words. How could I show LeRoy I revered him as the priest and prophet of our home?

Then I had read about how the prominent woman of Shunem built and furnished an upper room for Elisha, the holy man of God who often stayed with her family (2 Kgs 4:8-10).

She set up a bed, a table, a seat, and a candlestick for Elisha. Simple enough. But when I looked up the description of the furniture, I discovered the original word for stool or seat is the same used in other passages to designate a *throne*.[1]

Now putting away my folded towels, a thought kept running through my head. If the "man of God" who stopped off to visit in Shunem was treated to the best, shouldn't I treat the priest and prophet of our home likewise? Excitedly I called two friends and enlisted their help in setting up a "hubby corner" just for LeRoy. We lugged my study desk up to our master bedroom where I planned to create a special spot just for him. On it we placed a small lamp, his Bible, and some of his study books.

Over the desk I arranged a wall of his special mementos: his college diploma, a civic award, a decoupaged Scripture verse, and a small framed American flag presented to him after the astronauts returned from a Skylab launch on which he worked. This made the corner of our master bedroom uniquely his own.

But it lacked the "throne seat." My friends and I decided to bring his favorite green recliner from the den and set it beside his desk. Now he could do his leisure reading, leaning back undisturbed by the television or downstairs noises.

After supper that evening I found him sitting at the desk, writing checks to pay some bills and poring over a math problem he had to solve before morning. "Boy, this is really quiet and private. Thanks for doing this for me," he said, grinning.

Over the years, wherever we moved, we made him a special prophet's chamber, even if it is only a small corner of our master bedroom in our city apartment.

Setting up a special place for my husband seemed such a simple, insignificant thing to start with. But it has paid off in a bonus I never imagined because he knows I revere him each time he sits at the desk in his hubby corner, this prophet and priest of our home.

OTHER PROPHETS AND PRIESTS

What about other prophets and priests God might send our way? I mean, will they always wear a sign saying, "I'm a prophet" or "I'm a priest. Receive me."?

Jesus told his disciples plainly:

He who receives you receives me, and he who receives me receives the one who sent me. Anyone who receives a prophet because he is a prophet will receive a prophet's reward, and anyone who receives a righteous man because he is a righteous man will receive a righteous man's reward. And if anyone gives even a cup of cold water to one of these little ones because he is my disciple, I tell you the truth, he will certainly not lose his reward.   **Matthew 10:40-42**

It was Jackie Buckingham who shared this Scripture with me years ago when I was starting to open my home even to strangers in the body of Christ—with a bit of fear and reluctance, I admit. She explained her own early struggle, as related in her forward to this book.

"In fact, the first six months we lived in our house in the country, we entertained houseguests almost every night. That's when I stuck a 'Saved to Serve' sticker on the refrigerator." She laughed.

"But what did you do about the people, Jackie?" I asked.

"I got over resenting all these guests when I saw that promise in the Bible, in Matthew 10:41—that if I welcomed a prophet because he was a man of God, I would be given the same reward a prophet got. I took that to mean I would get a prophet's reward if I received a prophet, and a righteous man's reward if I received a righteous man. It changed my whole attitude."

"A prophet's reward? A righteous man's reward? Wow! But what if I don't have the provisions for all those who come to my house?" I asked Jackie.

"Go read about the widow of Zarephath and see how God blessed her when she received Elijah. You will get one answer there," she assured me.

So I did.

THE WIDOW OF ZAREPHATH

A famine was plaguing the land. Elijah had prophesied it as the word of the Lord. At first the ravens fed him, then the brook from which he drank dried up. God told him to go to Zarephath because he had *commanded* a widow to supply him with food.

As far as she knew, she was not providing for the prophet of God. She just busied herself gathering sticks, to make a fire and prepare one last meal for herself and her son before they died of starvation. Only a handful of flour and a little oil to make one cake—that is all she had.

At the town gate of Zarephath, the prophet Elijah called to her, "Would you bring me a little water in a jar so I may have a drink?... And bring me, please, a piece of bread" (1 Kgs 17:10b, 11b).

Elijah just did not understand. She had only enough for a final meal for herself and her son, she informed him. Unimpressed, the prophet instructed her to go make a small cake of bread for *him*. Then he directed her to make something for herself and son. "Don't be afraid," he encouraged.

This was a pretty bizarre instruction. A stranger telling her to feed him first, then herself. Did she hesitate? Did she know he was a prophet? Or did she simply obey out of curiosity? At any rate, God was in it. For the next words out of the prophet's mouth were reassuring:

> For this is what the Lord, the God of Israel, says: "The jar of flour will not be used up and the jug of oil will not run dry until the day the Lord gives rain on the land."
>
> She went away and did as Elijah had told her. So there was food every day for Elijah and for the woman and her family. For the jar of flour was not used up and the jug of oil did not run dry, in keeping with the word of the Lord spoken by Elijah. 1 Kings 17:14-16

That was not the end of her blessings. Later when this widow's son died, Elijah raised him back to life. She not only fed the prophet during the drought, she provided lodging for him too.

What a prophet's reward she received! Food throughout the famine. A miracle of life when death struck.

This widow of Zarephath (1) gave what she had, and (2)

God supplied abundantly in greater proportion than she ever gave.

She did not know *how* God would respond when she obeyed the prophet's order, she simply did what she was asked. She learned God's secret of *giving* and *receiving*.

TRUST GOD IN HARD TIMES

Whatever hard times we will face ahead, we must trust God to provide for us if we have been faithful to do what he's instructed us to do.

There may be days when we think our barrel—or pantry—is almost bare. We have to wholly depend on the Lord, giving him our needs, watching him provide. Sometimes he will supply supernaturally, perhaps by multiplying the food as he did when Jesus fed more than five thousand with two fish and five little barley loaves.

However, there may be times when God wants us to be prepared to feed our families and help our neighbor, friend, prophet, or even stranger. An example is Joseph who stored up grain during the years of plenty for the lean years God had warned him were coming. Because he did, his own family came to Egypt and was spared from starvation.

There is a Scripture that is worth considering since an economic earthquake is predicted: "Go to the ant, you sluggard; consider its ways and be wise! It has no commander, no overseer or ruler, yet it stores its provisions in summer and gathers its food at harvest" (Prv 6:6-8).

VILLAGE SPARED

When our friends George and JoAnne Bailey were in Europe they visited a village where a Christian woman took them down into the basement of her very old home. "I want to show you something," she coaxed.

"Food was once stored in all these copper bins. The Lord told my mother to stock food down here months before our country became involved in World War II. During the war, she fed almost our entire little village. The Lord just multiplied what she had faithfully stocked. We never went hungry," she told them. "The key to our survival was that my mother heard God, obeyed, and shared."

As JoAnne described the copper bins to me, she said the Lord had shown her that some American Christians need to be getting food stocked *now* so they can feed other people during coming times of lack. "There will be those who will hear God and be prepared to help others," she said.

"What kind of foods do you suggest?" I asked.

"Rice. Dried beans. And other foodstuffs that have a long shelflife. I put bay leaves in my bins of rice to keep down insects," she said.

"One other thing," JoAnne admonished us. "Time is moving fast. God is saying to me, 'I'm looking for some Abrahams who can stand and look out across the horizon and with one hundred percent trust, pack up and head out.' He is warning us, too, *Do not look back!*"

OUR BIBLICAL GRANDMOTHERS

Our "Biblical grandmothers" have set examples of hospitality for us. Let's consider lessons we can learn from several of them.

Sarah (Gn 18). Sarah, Abraham's wife, is the first woman recorded in the Bible to extend hospitality. She made bread cakes while her servants prepared a choice calf for Abraham to serve the three strangers who came with news from God that she—even in her old age—would conceive and bear a son. And of course she did, just as the visitors proclaimed.

Lesson to learn: Sometimes we will actually entertain heavenly visitors sent from God to deliver us a message. "Do not neglect to show hospitality to strangers, for by this some have entertained angels without knowing it" (Heb 13:2 NASB).

Rebekah (Gn 24). When Abraham sent his servant to seek a wife for his son Isaac, the servant prayed that he would be led to the one of God's choice. He even asked the Lord as a sign that she would not only give him water, but his camels also. When he came to the city of Nahor in Mesopotamia, he stopped for water. Rebekah, a beautiful virgin from Abraham's clan, came to the spring to draw water for her father's family. Seeing the stranger, she offered him water, and without prompting asked to water his camels also.

Humble, with a servant's heart, Rebekah did not view the needs of the animals as beneath her. Think how much water it took to satisfy ten thirsty camels! But these beasts were loaded with gifts—gifts she actually received after her hospitality. She agreed to return with the servant as Isaac's bride. Just imagine what she would have missed by not watering the camels—no Isaac for a husband.

Lesson to learn: Jesus said if we give even a cup of cold water, he will reward us. We do not give to receive a reward, but the Lord sees it, and he blesses us.

Queen Esther (Est 7). God will not only provide, he will protect us when guests come who are not coming in his name.

Esther gave a banquet and even invited her enemy. The beautiful Esther, queen of the Persian empire, could have lost her life along with all other Jews living in exile when her foster father, Mordecai, warned her of the impending danger.

A royal decree instigated by the wicked Haman had been

issued to kill all Jews. She was the only one close enough to the king to intercede. She and her maids agreed to join all the Jews in a three-day fast before she appeared before the king to appeal for mercy. Going to him was a dangerous procedure, since the king had not sent for her. But she had determined in her heart, "If I perish, I perish." So she approached him and invited him and his top executive, Haman, to a banquet, then the next day to another banquet.

There the king offered her even up to half his kingdom, but she revealed that she and her people were about to be slaughtered, annihilated—and the adversary was his own confidant, Haman. Haman's atrocious scheme was brought to light.

Enraged, the king ordered Haman executed and Esther's people were spared, with her foster father, Mordecai, promoted in the king's household.

Lesson to learn: From Queen Esther, a woman of courage, we learn discipline and balance. She did not rush into implementing a plan of her own but waited for her foster father's directions. Nor did she take a passive role and say, "If God wants to do something, he can do it." Also, she knew that right timing was imperative.

Rahab (Jos 2). Rahab hid the Israeli spies on her rooftop in Jericho. Thus she contributed to their first conquest in the Promised Land. When the battle was over, the walls of Jericho lay in a heap with all the inhabitants killed except for Rahab and her father's household—all spared due to her hospitality to the spies.

Rahab had initially told the spies that her people had heard how their Lord had dried up the Red Sea before they came out of Egypt. Just think, that miracle had occurred forty years earlier. The spies had agreed to let her live if she did not betray their mission. The red cord she hung from the window identified her house when the city was about to fall.

Lesson to learn: Sometimes we will be hospitable to people through whom we may later receive a reward. In this case, Rahab became not just a *hearer* of the God of miracles, but a follower after him. She is even mentioned later as the great-grandmother of King David and a shining example of faith. What a reward she received.

DIFFICULT PEOPLE

Sometimes we might extend hospitality to people who turn out to be our enemies. Laura learned the hard way to be careful whom she invited.

A woman had visited her church one Sunday and said she needed a place to stay while waiting for her house to be ready—some cleaning and painting needed to be done before the furniture arrived. The pastor and his wife, who knew of the woman's family, asked, "Laura, are you sure you want to have her?" But Laura, eager to serve the Lord through his people, replied, "Of course. We will do fine. It will be only a few days."

It was one of the most difficult situations she had encountered thus far. The woman was inconsiderate of everyone else. And when she left, she told the pastor terrible tales about how the Watsons had taken advantage of her—all lies.

But think of Judas, who for three years was in Jesus' inner circle of friends, yet was his betrayer. At Jesus' Last Supper with his disciples, he told them, "... one of you is going to betray me" (Jn 13:21b).

Once a spiritual leader—our closest confidant—turned against me personally, emotionally crushing me. One night I sat on the couch between LeRoy and Jamie Buckingham as they tried to comfort me. Finally Jamie looked me in the eye: "Quin, to whom much is given, much is required. Don't ever forget it." Then he prayed.

There will be people at our table who may in fact turn against us. If we know this is a possibility, it won't come as a shock. But remember that Jesus gave much to us—his very life. We can be hospitable for his sake and allow him to use (or turn) even bad situations into something for our good.

There is one more story in the Bible that sums up God's faithfulness to a homemaker who trusts him. Remember my reference from 2 Kings, when I was mulling over the Bible story of the prophet Elisha and the Shunamite woman? She had prepared a guest room for Elisha to stay in on his frequent visits to her area.

Elisha in return prophesied that God would give her a son. When the boy died from a heatstroke, Elisha performed a miracle in restoring him to life.

What blessing! All because she honored the man God sent her way with hospitality.

11

The Innkeepers

Cheerfully share your home with those who need a meal or a place to stay for the night.   1 Peter 4:9 TLB

FINDING A CAT shut up in my suitcase or a child dumping the contents of my purse no longer surprises me. Staying in private homes as I travel to speaking engagements has helped me learn to appreciate a good bed and meal, but not to get terribly upset with the unexpected. I do remember a time, though, when I almost lost my cool.

My friend Ginger and I had been on the road for three hours to reach this modern split-level farmhouse. Weary from four hours speaking at a women's seminar earlier in the day, I had looked forward to collapsing in bed, even without supper.

When I rang the doorbell, the wife, husband, and little boy all met us at the door. They just stood staring at us. Finally the wife spoke.

"Sorry, but I am not ready for houseguests yet. Could you

just come back later when I'm more organized?"

"Sure, we will go into town and eat. Then I'll call you from there," I said, trying hard to smile. "But would you care if we just checked into a motel? I don't mind taking care of the expense," I offered.

"Absolutely not. What would the women on our executive board think of me if you did that?" she replied.

Two hours later we returned. She told us we could sleep in the bed her son shared with his dog. She didn't change the sheets or make up his crumpled bed. Reluctantly he did come in and remove his hamster cage from beside the bed. Two beach towels were all we could find in the linen closet for our baths.

The next morning she admitted we were her first house-guests, but she had volunteered her home because it was new and she was an officer in the women's group where I was to speak. Thinking back to our own goofs, we laughed with her about her uneasiness and assured her we were flexible and forgiving.

However, this experience did make me more conscious of seeing that my own houseguests are provided with essentials to make their stays more comfortable.

MY BATH SURPRISE

On another speaking trip when Ginger drove me, we were housed in a large rambling two-story home. Spacious and tastefully decorated, it featured a bath complete with jacuzzi, sauna, shower and commodious dressing room. I insisted that Ginger pamper herself in those facilities since she had driven for the past twelve hours. Then, too, our hostess said there were other bathrooms down the hall.

That night when I sank into a warm tub of water in one of the smaller bathrooms, I was puzzled over the gritty sand on the bottom. Lathering up, I noticed the soap had a peculiar smell. When I spied the dish of food and water beside the tub, I realized I was sitting in the dog's bathtub, covered in flea soap.

"The dog's bathroom! Are you kidding me?" Ginger asked when I admitted my blunder while we were loading the car to leave the next day.

"So much for letting you have the best bathroom," I laughed as we drove away. "I wonder what our hostess thought when she discovered I'd even used Muffy's towel when I was a 'guest' in his canine tub?"

I have slept in upstairs attic rooms in Holland and Germany, and in a basement room next door to the noisy boiler in Brooklyn. But the situation in a New York suburb was the most intimidating.

The hostess in whose home I was scheduled to spend two nights hit me with a startling announcement as soon as my driver pulled away from the curb.

"I have a 'crazy' son living in the attic, an alcoholic son in the basement, and an unsaved husband who doesn't want you here because he has to sleep on the couch since I'm giving you our bedroom. But I volunteered because I love to be hospitable."

"Please be sure your family is in agreement before you invite me or any guest next time. I do not want to inconvenience your family, because this is their home," I told her. I tried my best to make other arrangements, but I had no choice but to spend both nights there.

In still another home there was no closet space in the room given me because ten years earlier the family's teenage son had stored his car parts there. The shell of the old car still sat abandoned in the carport.

But those are just my wide-eyed experiences. I have stayed in other places that made me positively purr with contentment.

BETTER BEDS

Once on a Georgia plantation I was given a bell to ring for a uniformed housekeeper to bring me breakfast in bed! But far more often I stay in "ordinary" homes with kids and friendly husbands who welcome me because they've learned to share what they have as part of their Christian hospitality.

Why do I stay in homes instead of motels? Because the organizations who invite me do not have funds for these. I have been pleased to form long time friendships and stay with some of these families on repeated visits.

HOMES I'M AT HOME IN

"Your room is ready whenever you want to come." I've heard that said by Elizabeth, Fran, Ginger, Laura, JoAnne, Bee, Jean....

JoAnne's house is a high-ceilinged 1930s military officer's quarters. Fran's is on a Florida lake. Ginger's is tucked into the woods. Laura's is an earth-sheltered house. Elizabeth's is on a canal and has a swimming pool. Jean's is atop a high Colorado mountain. I have stayed with Bee in their military housing in Germany, Ohio, and Florida. In every one of these I feel at home in "my room"—the place they prepare for me to stay whenever I visit them.

But what about people who are not really close friends? In Waukeegan, I was assigned to stay at Sharon's home three times. The night her husband came home with a "pink slip" after almost twenty years on the job, I was there to pray with him and Sharon with heart-felt compassion and love, like family.

When we lived on a Florida bayou that flowed into the Gulf of Mexico, it was not unusual for our friends with boats to dock at our back door. Several knew where we kept the house key and that they were welcome any time.

Returning home from a trip one Monday, we unlocked our back door and smelled the faint scent of bacon. "I'll bet Hilda and Hilliard came in their boat and cooked breakfast here," I told LeRoy. Sure enough, a note they left on the dining table thanked us for the use of our house over the weekend. How glad I was that they felt welcome, even when we were not home.

The *Encyclopedia Judaic* notes:

> In ancient Israel, hospitality was not merely a question of good manners, but a moral institution which grew out of the harsh desert and nomadic existence led by the people of Israel.... The Bible is replete with examples of pious hospitality.... One of Job's claims is that "the stranger did not lodge in the street, but I opened my doors to the traveler" (Jb 31:32 KJV).[1]

BE FLEXIBLE

JoAnne, wife of a military doctor, says if you have guests in your home, flexibility will save you from unnecessary trauma. She adds: "Make plans, but always be willing to change them.

"Once when George and I were stationed with the Air Force in Germany, we had fifteen people show up at our house for a several-day stay. It was not unusual to get a call from the train station in Weisbaden from someone saying a Christian family somewhere had told them our house would be a good stopover. We would set up pallets on the floor for the children, put the adults in beds. Sometimes George and I would go next door to our neighbor's house to sleep so a couple could have our master bedroom," she remembers.

From their experience, JoAnne and George offer these tips:

- Put good mattresses in your guest room.
- Esteem others more highly than yourself. See things from their perspective in planning meals, arranging the room.
- Pray over the room, that the guest will find peace and rest there. You might want to leave some Christian reading material on the bedside table.
- If you are hosting a guest speaker, allow them freedom to

study and prepare without having to spend all her time with your family members.

- On the other hand, if you are a guest speaker staying in a home and the meeting goes on until late at night, don't expect to be served a hot meal at two a.m. It is better to communicate in advance what your schedule will be and what the host and hostess will have available (and when it will be available) than to have misunderstandings later.
- Provide good balanced meals, not just what is easy for you to make. One guest speaker I know was served a chicken-broccoli casserole at five homes in a row because casseroles are easier to make ahead.

TEENAGE PARTY

My friend Ginger's slumber party for her teenage daughter Christen was a near disaster. Most of the girls showed a lack of consideration. Some helped themselves to Ginger's perfume, cooked on her stove at two a.m., spilled food and caused the fire alarm to go off, rummaged through dresser drawers and left her bathrooms in a mess, strewn with wet towels and soiled tissues.

Ginger came up with a few suggestions to pass on to her daughter:

- If you are a guest in a home, keep things neat and picked up for the host and hostess.
- Eat whatever is served with a grateful attitude.
- Offer to help afterwards with the dishes or small chores.
- Treat that home and family with the same consideration you would your own—respect them.

HOSPITALITY TO THE DISABLED

Fran, a nurse, has been married for over thirty years to her doctor husband, Mike. He has been in a wheelchair all their married life as a result of polio. Fran and Mike gave me some tips for considering houseguests with varied disabilities:

- Take up scatter rugs so a wheelchair will move more easily across the floor or so the elderly won't trip.
- Put a mat in the tub to prevent slipping.
- Ask if there are any special things needed to make it easier or more comfortable for your guest.
- Put a night light in the bedroom and bathroom.
- If a guest is diabetic, know what types of food he or she needs and the time they need to eat. They cannot be very flexible with meals, because diabetics are taking insulin and must balance food intake and insulin intake.
- Leave room at the table for the wheelchair, even if you have to rearrange some of the furniture.
- Disabled people need to be welcomed in more homes—it is refreshing for them to get out of their own familiar environment.

One holiday when a hearing-impaired college student was in our home for two weeks, I recognized that I needed to be more sensitive to people with limitations. If we did not play games she could easily understand, or if we did not stop all conversation and repeat slowly so she could read everyone's lips, she would react by running to her room.

Later I realized we needed to explain the general flow of conversation to her. However, it would not be fair to her or to the rest of us to allow her to manipulate us with her moods or put a guilt trip on us. The sensitive host would be cordial and forgiving. But let it be known that the guest "would be welcome to join in what the rest of the group is doing."

THE UNDEMANDING GUEST

Fran and Mike's home was a "hiding place" for Corrie ten Boom for a number of years. Corrie wrote several of her books propped up on her bed at their home. Fran remembers how she was never obtrusive, but she made known her needs. She liked a pot of hot tea at seven a.m. People wanted to serve her because she didn't demand.

"She would always ask me, 'What's on your schedule tomorrow, Fran?' out of consideration for our household plans. Corrie liked her short afternoon nap, and she awoke from ten minutes as refreshed as if she'd had eight hours of sleep. She loved wild flowers that her traveling companion Ellen often picked in the woods around our house. Corrie appreciated every little detail. She would always tell me to keep the furniture and pillows just like I had them, because when she came back it would be familiar and more like her very own room," Fran told me.

With a thoughtful hostess like Fran, it is easy to see why this delightful "tramp for the Lord" kept returning.

Francis Shaeffer, host to many on two continents, wrote:

> Pray that the Lord will send you the people of his choice. But don't pray that way unless, no matter who these people are across the whole board of the twentieth-century man, you are willing to take them into your home, have them at your table, introduce them to your family and let them sleep between your sheets. It is a day of no small games. We must have and practice an orthodoxy of community.[2]

THE HOST SETS THE MOOD

While most people like to feel "at home" when in another's house, it is up to the hostess/host to make them feel welcome. Fresh flowers are a nice welcoming touch. If nothing is blooming in your yard, most grocery stores sell cut flowers. This makes a guest feel you care about the details of their visit.

Laura looks around the edge of her property for wildflowers. "Brooks calls them blooming weeds, but I can make delicate, free-flowing arrangements with them. In fact, they seem to arrange themselves. I have several vases that fit especially well in our guest room, and I think fresh flowers have a way of saying 'Welcome.'"

My friend and often-coauthor Ruthanne Garlock points out that "Hospitality is a spiritual trait; entertainment is a worldly concept based on pride and greed." Ruthanne and her husband, John, a professor of missions at Christ for the Nations Institute in Dallas, have stayed in homes literally around the world. But she has learned a lot about the need for being hospitable wherever she hangs her hat.

"Flexibility will save you from unnecessary trauma," she has found. "Make plans, but always be willing to change them. I'm learning to be sensitive to the Lord's voice when things seem to go awry, to get his perspective on the situation.

"The difference in entertaining guests versus hospitality? Make people feel comfortable in your home, no matter how limited the budget. Give thought to your guests' comfort—especially those traveling a long time."

TIPS FOR HOSTS AND HOSTESSES

Ruthanne and John share their hints for making guests feel more at home:

- As soon as we arrive, show us our quarters and let us deposit our suitcases.
- Show us where the bathroom is, and tell us if we'll be sharing it with others (teens, small children, or adults). Show us where the towels and washcloths are.
- Provide space in our closet for our hanging bags and a few extra hangers.
- Provide glasses (and water) for the bedroom.
- Offer fruit juice or something refreshing when guests arrive.

- Let guests use laundry facilities or offer to wash clothes for travel-weary guests. Show us where the iron and ironing board are kept.
- The guest room should be arranged with a place for the suitcase—preferably not on the floor, if possible.
- In the bathroom, provide a hand mirror and wastebasket, towels, washcloths, soap, and toilet tissue (you would be surprised how many of these are missing, even in American homes).
- A mirror and a lamp of some kind in the guest room is a big help.
- Keep pets and children out of the guest's room (dog lies on bed, cat claws in suitcase, kids explore the contents of luggage...).
- Try to avoid awkward situations—like when a teenage son pops into the bedroom in the morning to get his clothes while a guest is still asleep.
- Take time to make guests feel they are not imposing.
- Respect guests' privacy. Do not play your radio or TV so loud that guests cannot sleep, pray, or study. For the sake of privacy—if possible—do not put your guest on a sleeper couch in the family room.

Ruthanne laughs about some of her experiences, especially when staying with families who do not speak English and they all make comical efforts to communicate. Ruthanne and John always take gifts to the family's children, which is a hit in any language.

"I want to be a blessing, not a burden when I am a house-guest," she said. "I do appreciate any little extras the family does for my comfort, and I've learned from them the warmth of special touches. Now I often put a bowl of fruit in the room when others stay in our home."

Francis Shaeffer points out: "There is no place in God's world where there are no people who will come and share a home as long as it is a real home."[3]

DO WITH WHAT YOU HAVE

The Lord may ask each of us to use our homes in a different way. With JoAnne's husband, George, an Air Force physician, they have moved a lot. Her house is furnished with what she calls "joyful junk." But every item reflects Jesus, from the stained glass window from Germany to a kneeling bench from an ancient church. She gives us some hospitality tips from varied experiences:

Sometimes when you feed the multitudes, you must put your hand on the pot and ask God to multiply and bless it!

I have a philosophy: do with what you have. If you have some of the finest china and silver and linen, use it. If not, improvise. If you do not have silver pieces for your table, use lots of baskets. If you do not have flowers, gather sticks, rocks, and leaves and make a centerpiece. Put rustic with rustic and fine with fine. But do use cloth napkins—they are quick and easy to iron. They say, "I care. You are special to me."

It takes time to be hospitable. Be rested and dressed when company comes. I prepare food ahead of time, but if I have a last-minute salad to put together, I am not intimidated if women gather in the kitchen to watch me. If I am comfortable, they will be comfortable. That means, do not attempt anything that is a burden to you—keep the menu simple. Whatever you feel good making is what you should serve."

Whenever I walk into the Baileys' front door, the house signals "Welcome!" JoAnne explains, "I spend a lot of time in prayer in my house, and it should reflect that. Whenever I expect company, I want them to feel I have prepared a place for them. Jesus has gone to prepare a place for us, so I treat my guests as him when I prepare a place for them in my home."

A wall plaque I saw says it well: *Let All Guests Be Received as Christ.*

12

Angels or Strangers?

Practice hospitality to one another—that is, those of the household of faith. (Be hospitable, that is, be a lover of strangers, with brotherly affection for the unknown guests, the foreigners, the poor and all others who come your way who are of Christ's body.) And [in each instance] do it ungrudgingly—cordially and graciously without complaining [but as representing Him]. 1 Peter 4:9 AMP

HURRYING TO FINISH the magazine article I was writing on hospitality, I resented the interruption of the phone ringing on the desk in my small home office.

"Hi, Quin. This is Sue," an unfamiliar voice greeted me. "We are vacationing in Florida and just can't wait to see you. We are down at McDonald's. Wonder if you could meet us and let us follow you to your house so we could visit?"

"How will I know you—I mean, recognize you, Sue?" I stammered, fishing for a clue.

"There are four of us. I will be behind the wheel of the yellow Cadillac with Texas license plates."

"Give me ten minutes." I prayed under my breath, "Lord, I do not have time for this interruption, and I sure do not have time for hospitality right now. Help!"

Thirty minutes later as we sat in our den sipping iced tea, I studied Sue's face. She must be LeRoy's cousin, I decided. Blond hair, blue eyes. Fits with all his German kin back in Texas.

This woman knew everything about us. Yet to me she was a complete stranger. She even knew the department at NASA where LeRoy worked as an engineer at Kennedy Space Center.

When LeRoy came in from work moments later and saw our four guests, he arched his eyebrows at me. I shrugged my shoulders. He did not know them either!

Smelling the chili simmering on the stove, Sue hinted that it must really taste good. I invited them to stay for supper. Running to the kitchen, I dumped three more cans of beans into the chili pot and made a large tossed salad. When our children and my mom joined us, we had ten around the table.

As we talked, I discovered they were now considering staying overnight with us. Inside I was more than irritated. I had that magazine article on hospitality to finish and mail by tomorrow. Though our home had been open to others for years now, tonight I just did not have time for hospitality—especially to strangers!

After supper Sue asked LeRoy to help them find some oranges and grapefruit they could pick. He took them down to Mother's backyard with several empty grocery sacks. I stayed home to clean up the kitchen and change bed linens.

An hour later he came back alone, saying they had decided to drive on a couple more hours that night, then stop in a motel.

"Did you ever find out who Sue is and how she knew so much personal information about us?" I quizzed him.

"Oh, yeah. She turned out to be my mother's hairdresser back in Bay City, Texas," he said, laughing loudly.

"Hairdresser? You must be teasing me."

"Yes, she was. For years, until Mom died this fall. Don't you women tell your hairdresser *everything*?" he said, his eyes rolling. "I guess Mom talked so much about us every week, Sue became very familiar with our family."

"Familiar? That's putting it lightly!" I groaned.

After I crawled into bed that night, I had a long talk with the Lord. He reminded me that for years my elderly mother-in-law had not been able to comb her hair properly with her crippled, gnarled, arthritic hands. Sue, her beautician, had in a sense been hospitable to her in a way I could not since we lived almost eight hundred miles away.

"Was three hours of your time and four bowls of chili given to strangers such a big sacrifice? Didn't I promise if you give even a cup of cold water in Jesus' name you will be rewarded?" the Lord seemed to ask.

"Lord, forgive me. My attitude was rotten, and my priorities were out of order," I admitted. The next morning I was up at daybreak finishing the manuscript with a whole new slant and a fresh illustration from my own life.

I have fed many strangers since Sue and her friends surprised me that long ago winter afternoon. The motivation: our pastor began asking church members to take visitors home with them for dinner following Sunday morning services. And we did, for a number of years.

CHRISTMAS CHALLENGE

However, there have been times when I still miserably flunked the hospitality test—I was not ungrudgingly hospitable.

One Christmas two of our children brought five of their classmates from Bible college home for the two-week holiday. One was a hearing-impaired girl, and the other four were from foreign countries. I loved having them and welcomed them with an open heart. We planned all sorts of fun things and encouraged them to cook their native dishes for us. We gave them presents for Christmas and let them phone their own families overseas to give them greetings.

One of the girls, however, had a real problem accepting our hospitality. She was an older student from northern Europe who had never visited in an American home before. A recent convert, she was horrified that we spent time in the evenings spread out on the floor playing games. She expected a prayer meeting every spare moment.

"We are told to pray without ceasing. Why are you playing silly games?" she shouted at me.

I tried to explain that we were not a television-watching family, and we found that playing games together brought us some enjoyment. We did have prayer times, and she had been part of those. But evenings before a roaring fire was a fun time to play games.

When I took her to the shopping mall, she disappeared. I found her laying hands on a crippled baby while the child's startled mother tried to intervene. She shoved Christian tracts at sales clerks, and even kneeled in the middle of the mall to pray, drawing shoppers' curiosity.

As the days progressed, she wore on my patience. I found myself reacting to her criticism about our family's way of living. She poked at me by quoting Scripture, trying to make me look absolutely ridiculous.

I was distraught. Two weeks of time alone with my own children would have been nice. Instead, we were giving up our privacy to provide a home for strangers.

My pity party continued.... She complained and tried to start arguments, even with the other students. Pouting, she went to bed ahead of us.

After she was asleep, the rest of us prayed for God to show us ways to express his love to her.

First, I had to ask the Lord to forgive me. He sent her, I decided, to expose my own heart's need for cleansing. Had she been Jesus Christ himself—the living, laughing, loving Lord—I would not have treated him the way I did her. I repented, and I asked her to forgive me.

When they left, she hugged me reluctantly. "You do have a good heart. I learn many lessons here...." Her attitude against authority eventually got her expelled from Bible school. After probation, she was allowed to return and graduate.

GOD'S CHOICE PEOPLE

In her book *Be My Guest*, Vivian Hall explains how her family makes their guest room available to fellow Christians needing a place to stay when they are in her city. Often they are strangers. Yet she can think of no single instance when she had to refuse someone because of lack of room or physical strength to care for them. When you decide on this type of hospitality, this is what she says you are asking God to do for you:

- To send the people of his choice
- To choose the time they should come and to decide how long they should stay
- To protect you from those who would misuse your hospitality
- To give you spiritual insight to know how to meet both the physical and spiritual needs of your guests
- To keep your own spirit open to the blessings God has planned that you receive from these guests

Vivian says, "I can say emphatically that God has never failed us in any of these areas. Because we have found him so dependable it has become more and more enjoyable to participate in the ministry of hospitality. When we have chosen to obey, our blessings have far outweighed the effort that we have expended."[1]

Now, when our phone or doorbell rings, rather than viewing it as an interruption, I wonder if the Lord might be sending me another opportunity to practice hospitality, even to a stranger.

John commends this attitude in his third epistle:

Beloved, you do faithfully whatever you do for the brethren and for strangers, who have borne witness of your love before the church. If you send them forward on their journey in a manner worthy of God, you will do well. **3 John 5-6 NKJV**

Study notes on 3 John in *The Spirit Filled Life Bible* state: "This letter portrays the church as a family united by bonds of love with its members extending gracious hospitality toward one another." Another note says that "Those who support missionaries share in their work of the gospel."[2]

Laura and Brooks hosted a German couple from an area that had been behind the Iron Curtain. They were Christians (Moravians) on the first trip they were allowed outside the former East Germany.

The Watsons were concerned that these lovely people feel comfortable in such a strange environment. The husband, an engineer, spoke passable English. But his wife Sigrid understood only "hello" and "thank you."

However, as they were leaving, Sigrid asked Laura's friend Rita, who speaks German, to translate for her. The message: "We couldn't communicate in our languages, but we communicated very well with our hearts."

"I don't know when I have been so blessed," Laura says, with a tear in the corner of her eye. "It was like God had smiled on us."

But, as Laura reminds me, sometimes even the most welcome guests can bring unsettling circumstances in their baggage.

This literally happened to Laura. Her grandson James walked through her back door last spring and said, "Grandmom, meet my friend C.J." Wrapped around his arm was a baby python!

Laura's eyes nearly popped out of her head. Grinning, James explained, "'Camouflage Jake, the Ranger Snake' is C.J.'s full name. He's the mascot of Ranger Company of Georgia Tech's R.O.T.C. Somebody had to take care of him during spring break, so I volunteered. He will sleep very quietly in his little canvas bag."

Somehow God gave Laura grace to smile through even this "guest." Grandparents will put up with a lot.

ANGELS OR STRANGERS?

Sarah, our first Biblical "grandmother" who was hospitable, made bread cakes for three strangers who passed their tent in the heat of the day. The Bible account implies that these strangers were angels. Later on in the Bible we are told, "Do not neglect to show hospitality to strangers, for by this some have entertained angels without knowing it" (Heb 13:2 NASB).

I never read that Scripture verse without thinking of an incident that happened a few years back to Marie, a pastor's wife, when they welcomed a stranger in tattered clothes to a picnic behind their parsonage. Marie told me about it:

It was in the evening and we had the youth fellowship from our church for a cookout in our backyard. While they were singing and having a good time, we noticed this man standing over in the shadows. I remember Charlie went over to him and invited him to come share our food and have a drink of hot chocolate. The kids were cooking hot dogs over an open fire.

The man said he did not want anything to eat. He had heard the singing and had come closer to hear it better. But, he told me, he would take a glass of cold water, if I did not mind. The three of us—he, Charlie, and I—walked back to the house.

I went in and got him a glass of water to drink. We started to walk back to the young people—Charlie walking beside him. Then it seemed we got a bit ahead of the stranger, sort of leading him to the group.

All of a sudden he was not there. We ran to the street and looked toward the highway that ran past our street. But he was not in sight. The street in front of our house was wide—there was no place this man could have just disappeared to in that short time. How could he walk off so quickly?

Who was this stranger to whom Marie offered a glass of cold water in Jesus' name? A tramp? An angel? Marie will never know. But she, like Sarah, was willing to share what she had with a stranger. Just a cup of cold water, given in love, is an acceptable act of hospitality. Both to a guest and to God. Such a simple thing, but worthy.

PRAYERFULLY INVITE

All are not angels. Some are just strangers. How do we know whom to invite? We read in the second epistle of John:

Many deceivers, who do not acknowledge Jesus Christ as coming in the flesh, have gone out into the world. Any such person is the deceiver and the antichrist. Watch out that you do not lose what you have worked for, but that you may be rewarded fully. Anyone who runs ahead and does not continue in the teaching of Christ does not have God; whoever continues in the teaching has both the Father and the Son. If anyone comes to you and does not bring this teaching, do not take him into your house or welcome him. Anyone who welcomes him shares in his wicked work.   2 John 7-11

When we got into the flow of hospitality, we learned we had to be careful who we invited. I once let Mike, our first "adopted" son, bring home a young ex-drug addict who turned out to be a regular con artist. And there was the young man LeRoy tried to help who later hanged himself in jail. What spirits had we allowed into our home? Were these people God-sent, or emissaries of the enemy?

We began to pray: "Lord, who do you want in our home? Who are we to minister to? To feed? To clothe? To shelter?"

Just as Jesus did nothing without first asking the Father, especially in these uncertain times we need his direction and some discernment.

I heard a pastor say, "You do not have to be the answer to every need you see. You might rob someone else of an opportunity. But if you are the one to respond, do it heartily as unto the Lord."

Some Old Testament hospitality rules were explicit: "The alien living with you must be treated as one of your native-born. Love him as yourself..." (Lv 19:34a).

We are familiar with the story of the widow Ruth who gleaned for food from Boaz's fields in Bethlehem. Farmers were required by law to leave the corners of their fields to be harvested by the poor. In Deuteronomy 24:19 we read: "When you are harvesting in your field and you overlook a sheaf, do not go back to get it. Leave it for the alien, the fatherless and the widow...." Also see Leviticus 19:9 and 23:22.

Jesus himself said when you give a banquet, "... invite the poor, the crippled, the lame, the blind, *and you will be blessed*" (Lk 14:13b-14a italics mine).

There will be times God wants us to be hospitable to those who cannot invite us back. We need to pray about who to reach out to, who to help.

But there is no need to get so frazzled that you are no earthly good to your family and others. So find a balance in ministering to others.

OUR RESPONSE

God does not always confront us with "thus saith the Lord," but he does arrange our circumstances so we find ourselves responding to situations orchestrated by him.

We have pain, and he uses the time to test us. We find some people cause us dismay—they goad us into seeking the Lord on our knees. Here too come those who understand our need—they encourage us not to falter.

We seek guidance, and the Lord sends a variety of people our way. Each with a piece of the puzzle which, when they are all fit together, will make a picture of our life's opportunity to magnify him.

We have joy, and he shows us that this is his nature. Our joy is multiplied as we share it with those who need to feel the healing touch of his love; we are doubly blessed as we minister to them.

Then we can discern the pattern he is using to mold us to conform to his likeness and, like Paul, can "give thanks in all circumstances, for this is God's will for you in Christ Jesus" (1 Thes 5:18).

Someone has said that hospitality does not seek to impress—but to serve. Hospitality does everything without thought of reward, but the pleasure of giving, loving, serving. Our churches are filled with strangers who need love.

With all this in mind, our response can be, "Lord, send the people of your choice to my house."

For I was hungry and you gave me something to eat, I was thirsty and you gave me something to drink, I was a stranger and you invited me in, I needed clothes and you clothed me, I was sick and you looked after me, I was in prison and you came to visit me.   **Matthew 25:35-36**

13

Singular
Hospitality

God setteth the solitary in families: he bringeth out those which are bound in chains: but the rebellious dwell in a dry land. Psalm 68:6 KJV

NOT ALL HOME HOSPITALITY FITS into a couples category. The circumstances of singles are quite different. Are they young or old? Have they ever been married? Divorced? Widowed? Do they have children? A growing number of young adults are rejecting stereotype labels society once hung on them. Many who have chosen to stay single longer are saying, "Being unmarried is not a tragedy but an opportunity to develop and be used of the Lord in a different measure."

How is the church going to meet their needs and utilize their talents more fully?

Jim Smoke, president of a ministry to single adults (Growing

153

Free) and director for the Center for Divorce Recovery, has been called the father of single adult ministry. In their book *Single Adult Passages*, Carolyn Koons and Michael Anthony quote extensively from Smoke. His vision for singles includes:

- Single adults will constitute the greatest field for evangelism in the next decade.
- Ministry to singles has become as important to church life as any of its ministries.
- Outdated doctrines concerning divorce and remarriage deserve another look—many were based on misguided interpretation of Scripture.
- Ministry to singles, regardless of their marital status, should include their children.[1]

In addition, Koons and Anthony note: *"many singles will find themselves classified as 'terminally poor.'* The theme song of some singles—'Don't worry, be happy'—can later translate into financial insecurity."[2]

Yet some of the most gracious hosts and hostesses I know are single—including coeds, career men and women, single parents, widows, and widowers.

EXEMPLARY WOMEN

Janis is one who comes to my mind right away. A school-teacher, Janis shared a rental house with Linda, another teacher, and Debby, a dental hygienist. Their little house was the scene of frequent covered-dish suppers for the college and career-age men and women from their church. "Having covered-dish suppers was about the only way we could afford hospitality with crowds," Janis told me. "We did love to get together at our house to talk and sing and eat. It's the friendship that's really important."

Quinett and Sharona, alone one Sunday after church, decided

not to let the lack of male companionship stop them from having fun. Packing a picnic basket with their very best—two china plates, two crystal goblets, two settings of sterling silverware—they set out their lunch on wicker bed trays in an exclusive garden park in Dallas.

They really enjoyed their chicken and potato salad lunch. People strolling through the park stopped to chat. "What a novel idea!" said a woman from England. "Reminds me of the continent." "Where are the young men who could be enjoying this with you?" asked another.

Elaine, a youth worker, says their career crowd beats the high cost of entertaining by having "bring your own" cookouts. Each person provides his or her own steak (or hamburger) and potato for the outdoor grill. The hostess prepares the salad, beverage, dessert, and furnishes paper plates, cups, and flatware. Each guest then puts fifty cents to one dollar in a kitty to reimburse the hostess for her expenses.

They also have brown-bag parties with each guest bringing a sack lunch to eat around a beach bonfire or an apartment swimming pool. Once when it rained they moved the picnic into a living room and listened to records on the stereo while eating from their brown bags.

"The young men cannot afford to take girls out as much as they would like, but we've found they do not mind bringing something over to our apartment and helping us girls to cook it. Some of the best parties we have happen when eight to ten guys and gals from the church get together in our kitchen to cook a meal. We all pitch in afterwards to clean up, too," Elaine said.

Picnics, outdoor barbecues, buffet suppers—the ideas are limitless. But young unmarried women should be sensitive about putting men on the spot by asking them out in a manner that comes across as forward, aggressive, out-to-trap-you. I know of a single young man who hesitated to even give a young woman a ride home from church because of her approach and saucy attitude when she asked for the ride.

Once a young schoolteacher was a dinner guest at our house.

She cornered one of our "sons" and said, "You will be a good catch for someone." He blushed. We have never invited her back, because she makes all the single men uncomfortable with her come-on attitude.

MEN ARE HOSPITABLE, TOO

David Johnson, a single Christian, made a habit of inviting company every Sunday to his table while he was an accountant. "I had married couples and singles over and over again, because I enjoy cooking and expressing hospitality. But not *one* of the married couples ever invited me to their home," David said wistfully. At the time of our conversation he was cooking supper at our apartment for some new Bible school students tired of cafeteria food.

Greg says he likes to have a "collective party" as he calls it. That means three or four others help with preparations. "This leads to friendship, true 'camaraderie.' I plan simple, not expensive meals—and I like to cook out. Regardless of what people think, guys are no different from gals in that we *do* like to be hospitable too."

Some singles with families find they don't have the time to entertain, much less the money. It was author JoAnn Sekowsky who brought this to my attention so keenly.

"Singles and hospitality do not go together nearly enough," JoAnn told me. "One of the big problems that holds so many back from being more hospitable is their impossible situation of being mother-father-breadwinner all at once. There just is not time to expend on hospitality under the circumstances."

JoAnn says that being single seems to be such a shattering experience for women—such an ego-destroying process—that far too many of them are not confident enough to open their houses to others.

Dottie was one of these. Following a painful divorce, her self-esteem hit a new low. When a friend offered her a part-time job, she hesitated to take it: "I can't do anything." But she was wrong—she proved herself by learning computer skills.

Then she joined a small prayer group from her church, and this provided supportive new friends.

Dottie is one of a group of ten friends who gather weekly for tea to relax a while and enjoy the company of good friends. Dottie was hesitant about this, saying, "I don't like to cook (though her chocolate cheesecake is ooh-la-la), but the group is welcome to come here any time if they will bring the refreshments."

No problem: (1) Dottie always contributes something luscious; (2) her apartment is so tastefully furnished that everyone loves an excuse to go there.

Now it is not just women friends she invites to her place. A home group of singles often meets there, and she gives dinner parties that include couples as well as singles.

Dottie's self-esteem is now firmly fixed. As she has experienced love and acceptance from friends, she has blossomed into an outgoing, vivacious lady.

I know two single women with children who open their homes on Saturday night. Nothing formal, just for chatting and fellowship. They tell me their single friends like to come to a home on a regular basis and do not mind bringing refreshments with them. What they appreciate is an open home where they can come to talk and share and yes, sometimes to pray for one another.

Another single friend, very limited in income, simply serves lemonade and bowls of popcorn to her invited guests. But she makes the party so much fun people love to go to her "popcorn fests."

ONE-PARENT HOMES

Betty, a working mother in a one-parent home, is an especially hospitable hostess. She has as many as four married couples at once to her home for a sit-down dinner. She says she enjoys using her china, silver, crystal, and candles when she has company. Last year her house was home base for the single women in her church who came together on a regular basis once a month. Several times she invited some of us married couples to join the singles for covered dish suppers and prayer time.

Recently God showed Betty she is to invite each of the church elders and their wives over to her home for dinner, so she will get to know them better. One day she read that she was to "... know them which labour among you and are over you in the Lord..." (1 Thes 5:12b KJV).

"How can I really know those who are in spiritual authority over me unless I invite them into my home? There is just something about sitting down to dinner together that brings people closer," she told me. I thought it was a splendid idea.

Right inside the doors of a cafeteria chain in Texas where we sometimes eat is posted a sign: "Any loners wanting company sit where the sign says, FRIENDSHIP TABLE." At least half a dozen tables are designated "Friendship Table." They told me this was a new policy. Mainly it is the senior citizens who take advantage of it.

WIDOWS

It seems particularly hard for a widow to get back into the swing of entertaining after her husband's death, for, after all, half of her is missing.

One widowed friend began her social life again by inviting another couple who had been close friends for years to help her co-host a dinner party. She asked the husband in particular to keep the men's conversation flowing. After several parties with her closest friends acting as "back-up hosts," she was finally comfortable hosting a party on her own. But she says it was rocky going for a while.

After thirty-five happy years of marriage, Rita lost her husband Don to lung cancer. But instead of staying in her house, dwelling on the past, in four months she had gone back to her part-time job and to taking friends out to dinner. "Why should I sit home and be morbid? The goal of every Christian is to go to heaven; I would never want my husband to come back from heaven. So I go on living one day at a time, as I know Don would want me to," she said.

Of course there were tears in her eyes when Rita talked about Don. But her friends have been considerate to include her in their varied plans. Herein lies a challenge for every Christian. We need to look around for the recently bereaved, the lonely, the unloved, and include them and other single adults when we have get-togethers.

Dot Burns, a widow for over twenty years, is one of the most hospitable people Laura and I know. We always are sure, when we are travel-weary, if we can but make it to Birmingham we will have a bed waiting. We look forward to that feather comforter she will wrap us in.

Dot is one of those people with whom we can be totally ourselves. She will love us no matter what our mood, and we are never an inconvenience. Our children feel free to drop in, too— my daughter Quinett was passing through at two a.m. one time, but Dot was genuinely glad to see her. Laura once called her at six a.m. on a Saturday from Dallas where she'd been for her father-in-law's funeral.

"Dot, Brooks wants to go home through Atlanta, but that is too far for one day's drive as tired as we are. Could we spend the night with you?"

"Come on. I'd love to see you."

When they got in at 10:30 that night, it was as though she had been preparing for weeks for them. The table was already set for breakfast the next morning.

I have dropped in many times, even with a carful of friends; she put us in her special basement apartment she created just for guests. She calls it her "Prophet's Chamber."

We love to go there because she is a hostess in the best Southern tradition, using her fine china and silver platters that have been in the family for years.

What a difference between Dot and Eula, also a twenty-year widow. Eula, living in the same state, told me she has never served a meal in her large dining room. Instead of people, she filled it with china cabinets to house her three complete sets of fine china.

"Even when my husband died, family who came for the funeral did not go in there. Somehow it is just a museum for me," she said. She told me I was one of the first persons outside her family to ever spend the night in her large home. However, she did let me and her sister pray for her to open her heart and her home to those God would send.

Isabelle bought a tiny house in Florida to be near her son. She chose it because it had one advantage: a large outdoor swimming pool. Every Sunday afternoon it is full of Vietnamese relatives of her daughter-in-law. "I let them swim as my 'outreach' ministry for Jesus, since many of them were brought up in the Buddhist faith back in Asia," she told me.

La Clair, my recently retired ninety-one-year-old neighbor, has young people from kindergarten to Bible school age knocking on her door to chat or share a snack. She still drives herself to church and the beauty shop. But in our school community complex, it is her cozy apartment where the young like to gather to draw from her wisdom and wit.

There is no limit to the creative opportunities open to a widow with an anointed imagination. Elvera Denning wrote to *Focus on the Family* magazine that her home is in one of West Virginia's beautiful "hollars," and it is open to Christian families needing a rest.

"My library of two thousand tapes and books are available for anyone who can tear themselves away from watching the deer and listening to the frog concerts."[3]

TEENAGERS

Teenagers are another group with special needs. They often feel left out when it comes to entertaining their friends at home. They seem to think they have to go somewhere—to a theater, a bowling alley, a pizza parlor—when, in fact, a home is the ideal place for them to bring their friends.

One of the most fun-for-teens parties we helped with was a progressive supper for thirty-two young people at Christmas time when our daughter Quinett was a high school senior. The kids planned to go to Nancy's for the salad course, Julie's for dessert, but to our house for the main course.

Quinett literally "decked the halls with boughs of holly," fresh pine branches, tapered candles, and crepe paper streamers. Our entire downstairs sang with the colors and fragrance of Christmas. The young folk decided they wanted it to be a dress-up occasion, so most of the girls who did not already have one, made simple long holiday dresses for themselves.

I did not know many of those who were coming since they were mostly school friends, not the kids from the church who were always popping in. The week of the party I prayed daily, a prayer I scribbled in my prayer notebook: "Lord Jesus, you went to a wedding, a feast, and a banquet. May the banquet we have for Quinett be one you could come to, too."

The big night came. Quinett slipped into her long blue gown and took off for Nancy's to meet the others there for salad. An hour later she called to let me know it was time for us to dish up the food.

LeRoy carved the turkey and he and Lib helped me arrange 32 plates with dressing, cranberry sauce, green beans, potatoes, and gravy. Moments later the teens came bursting in the door. LeRoy gathered them in the living room, asked God's blessing on the food and their friendship, and invited them to sit at one of the five tables we set up in the downstairs rooms.

Then he helped me serve them. "You take the living room

tables," LeRoy called as he balanced a big tray of plates over his head to squeeze into the dining room where most of them were seated.

After they ate, he also helped me clear the tables so the teenagers could linger to talk. They sang a few songs around the piano, went caroling across the street, then headed for Julie's for dessert and games.

Our part of the party had gone smoothly. I was pleasantly surprised at the number of thank-you notes we received the next week, many of them from the boys. God had honored my prayer. It was the kind of banquet Jesus could come to.

"Let's do it again next Christmas," Quinett begged. "OK, if you do the cooking!" I teased. Actually, she had hosted many parties at our house; this was one of the few my husband and I had been privileged to serve for her and her friends.

When it comes to throwing a party that teenagers love, I don't know a more versatile nor more energetic hostess than Mayanne (mother of four handsome and extremely popular sons). She thinks God has given her a specific opportunity to minister to teenagers through her home. "I try to remember that our home may be the only Christian home some young people are ever exposed to."

Mayanne plans each party around a theme, checking with her sons first for their approval. Once she had a "tacky party" where she asked the kids to come dressed as hobos. She ladled their camp stew into individual tin cups, served their beverage in old fruit jars and tied the silverware in napkins on a hobo stick. The kids sat out under the stars laughing the night away as they commented on how ridiculously tacky they had dressed.

"You have to give teens foods they are familiar with and that are easy to serve in a relaxed atmosphere," she said.

PREPARE PLENTY!

Since hospitality is an art to be developed, we are all bound to make mistakes along the way. This may be especially true for young people who cannot yet imagine how much food it takes to feed the crowds they invite.

One Sunday night the college fellowship asked if they could use our house for their after-church get-together. All they wanted me to furnish was the punch. They assured me they would bring plenty of refreshments. Imagine my dismay when sixty-seven young adults showed up but brought enough food to feed only half the crowd!

Two plates of sandwiches disappeared during the first few minutes they were set on the buffet. One little chocolate sheet cake served only twelve hungry mouths. Three bags of chips with dip lasted a little longer. A scrumptious lemon meringue pie sent dozens of people to the kitchen for a fork to get a stab at it. In the meantime, I was in the kitchen making up four giant bowls of punch, hoping to satisfy some thirsty appetites.

One Christmas holiday a group of single women invited five married couples who had provided prayer support and counseling to them through the year for a covered dish supper as a token of thanks. When the singles arrived and spread their food on the buffet, there was very little rib-sticking food. The hostess who headed up the singles' group blushed with embarrassment as she arranged the tiny serving dishes. One of the wives sensed her dismay and slipped an arm about her waist. "It is not your fault. They just are not used to cooking for a crowd. But look at all those yummy desserts. We can fill up on them."

Then with a smile she said, "I have learned in the course of doing I will make mistakes. But I cannot get discouraged. I must pick myself up, take a deep breath and start over. It gets easier, believe me. Look at this as a learning experience for all of us."

The next year they had the most delightful covered dish supper you could imagine—with lots and lots of nourishing food.

Most singles I talk to agree that a cooperative dinner party makes for a minimum of work and expense, yet provides one of the most rewarding fun evenings possible. Teenagers and single women are not the only ones who underestimate the amount of food needed; married women make mistakes too. But experience teaches all of us who are practicing hospitality to "prepare plenty."

Doubles, take note: Doubles, let me remind you of your own obligation to recognize singles as individuals who need relationships with you, too.

Vivid in my memory is the experience of one of my closest friends who had been part of a group of married couples for some years. Then her husband died. After a while of genuine, loving concern, the rest of the group went on to do their "couples" things. Without her. Understandable, but it hurt to be left out, alone.

Then there was the group Laura and Brooks led for several years. It started with four couples. We invited one of our close friends to join us, and later another one. Both singles. One was a widow and one a divorcée. Their presence among us caused the rest of us to look at ourselves as individuals—actually the way God sees us, too. This took nothing away from the couples' togetherness. In fact, it made us see our mates in a different light, and it was healthy.

Loys Mundy, who is a single missionary, zeroed in on this kind of thing in a letter:

> When a family comes home, they come as a team. They have one another's support and help in times of adjustment, househunting, making new friends. A single comes alone. So a note of caution—try not to show preference for couples/ families versus those of us who are single. We are on the team with you all who stay by the stuff at home, whether single or married. And we need each other. I praise God for the couples who do take singles like me under their wings and include us in their families. Singles need to be with other singles, yes; but we need the balance which couples and families can bring as well.

Singles, take note: I have a challenge for you, too, singles: Clear another night on your calendar and find a group or home church of mostly couples to plug into. You will find encouragement and stability there, and acceptance as well.

PART FOUR

Blessings of Sharing

14

Who Will "Titus" Me?

Older women likewise are to be reverent in their behavior, not malicious gossips, nor enslaved to much wine, teaching what is good, that they may encourage the young women to love their husbands, to love their children, to be sensible, pure, workers at home, kind, being subject to their own husbands, that the word of God may not be dishonored. **Titus 2:3-5 NASB**

THE BIBLE IS EXPLICIT that the older women are to train the younger women. Today we call this principle "mentoring." It does not matter whether the women are older or younger chronologically, married or single. Mentoring is the passing down of knowledge and training from one who is more experienced to one who is less experienced.

Mentoring is the involvement of one person in the welfare of another so that potentialities of the other are developed to their optimum capacity. A mentor encourages his followers to do the work better than the mentor can, says Ted Engstrom.[1]

While older women are admonished to train, it is the younger women who must ask for help, sometimes a humbling act.

TRAIN THE YOUNGER WOMAN

I remember one of the first times I was asked to help. A young mother named Dale, whom I barely knew, called me after I'd taught a hospitality class.

"I would like to use our small apartment for Christian ministry. But I am a poor housekeeper, and I certainly do not know how to cook well enough to have guests in to eat. Can you come help me?" Dale was calling on the phone after hearing me speak to the women of our church on basic hospitality etiquette.

She admitted that she had not learned basic homemaking skills as a youngster. As a teenager she had married an airman, moving with him to several bases. But she never took time—or felt competent enough—to open her home for Christian fellowship.

The next morning when I walked into Dale's neat little apartment and found it already immaculately clean, I realized Dale was a good housekeeper, fairly well organized and, I suspected, a decent cook. What she lacked was self-confidence in her own abilities.

As she rocked her year-old baby, she read to me from a scribbled list of things she wanted to learn.

- How to properly set a table and serve guests
- How to prepare economical company meals
- How to make her master bedroom prettier (the bedspread and curtains clashed horribly)

- How to be a good mother yet have more time for herself and her husband.

It did not take me long to discover the last thing on her list was her most pressing need. She allowed her baby to wear her out. Whenever the baby fretted, Dale nursed her. There was no regular nap time; by allowing the baby to stay up late, she and her husband had little time alone. While she cleaned house, the baby was either on the floor beside her or jostled on Dale's hip. No wonder she had no free time for herself!

I suggested she put the baby to bed in the afternoons for play or sleep and get some rest herself. I also urged her to put the baby to bed earlier at night, so she and her husband could have some quality togetherness time.

As the baby crawled at our feet, Dale and I went through the basic routine of setting the table—putting silverware and napkins in proper order. We even practiced serving imaginary guests their plates. "Serve from the left, remove plates from the right," I instructed her. Rummaging through her cupboard, we found an appropriate centerpiece for her dining table. But she did not own a tablecloth, so we decided to make one out of a twin-size sheet.

I promised to mail her some budget-stretching recipes. Since she liked to cook Italian and Mexican dishes, I suggested she serve those when she had guests—she would be comfortable with the familiar.

Next we evaluated her master bedroom. How depressing it must be to wake up in a room with such wildly contrasting floral patterns. "Let's ask God to give you the right curtains and bed-spread to replace these," I said, knowing full well her household budget would not allow her to buy new ones.

Just before I left, Dale committed her home to the Lord, asking him to use it as a tool for hospitality ministry.

The next day she called, excitement echoing in her voice. "Guess what? We had a drop-in guest for supper last night. I only had chicken livers and rice with a salad, but I prepared our plates at the kitchen stove and served our meal at the table like a real hostess."

Mark up a victory for Dale and God, I thought. Then I shared my good news: my mom had some soft pastel curtains and a matching bedspread she wanted to give her—pink tones that would make her bedroom look soft, inviting, peaceful.

Dale was delighted. So was her husband the next week when the bedroom had its new decor in place. Dale eventually got the courage to have more than one airman at a time at their table. By the time her next baby was born, she put him on a schedule and allowed time for herself and her husband.

FIRSTHAND LOOK

Not long after Dale's phone call, Lucy (a mother of four young children) who had attended the same hospitality seminar, called me.

"May I come out to your house to see how a real home should look? I need help and ideas," she explained. "I don't even know how to set a table properly. With nine kids in our family, we had to take turns eating and only had jars for glasses. Mother did not teach us any social graces, and I have felt handicapped all my married life."

The next day as I showed Lucy through our house, I pointed out inexpensive ways to decorate on a budget—framing greeting cards, using things I already had for wall hangings such as china plates, a quilt, and a matted, framed lace doilie. I gave her my favorite "busy mama" recipes, many of them passed on to me years earlier by older women in my church.

It really freed her when she realized that I did not have fancy china or expensive silverware. I use plain white dishes but have a variety of colorful tablecloths made from sheets. Much of my furniture is hand-me-downs or garage sale purchases.

"People want to come to a warm home, not for the decor or

the food, but for the love," I told her.

Lucy grew in her confidence and ability, inch by inch, until finally at her husband's urging, she was ready to open her home for a weekly Bible study. Whenever she was discouraged, she called and asked me to pray with her. I kept up with her for years either by letter or phone as they moved to other localities.

Hans Rookmaaker, Dutch art professor and founder of a Dutch L'Abri community, differentiates between students (taught ones) and disciples (trained ones). He believes that a student learns everything a teacher teaches. But a disciple goes beyond that, taking the teacher's ideas and building on them.[2]

HELP EACH OTHER

Both Peter and Paul had something to say about helping each other.

"God has given each of you some special abilities; be sure to use them to help each other, passing on to others God's many kinds of blessings," wrote Peter (1 Pt 4:10 TLB).

Paul told the Ephesians: "Why is it that he gives us these special abilities to do certain things best? It is that God's people will be equipped to do better work for Him, building up the church, the body of Christ, to a position of strength and maturity" (Eph 4:12 TLB).

I remember when our pastor had all of us "register" our individual talents at the church office so that if someone needed the skills we had, we could call on the someone gifted in that area to share them.

My talent was for writing, so I taught writing classes at the church. But because bread baking was not my expertise, I wanted my daughters to learn from the best. So I went with Sherry while Margaret taught us how to mix and knead. We spent all day, kneading and kneading, and enjoying the aroma of bread baking.

EARLY BIBLICAL TRAINING

In Bible times, the Hebrew mother shared the responsibility for training her children. At the proper age, the sons went with their fathers to work, while the mother turned her attention to her daughters more fully. She taught them how to be successful wives and mothers—homemakers.

Often a daughter married at an early age and her mother-in-law stepped in to continue the training her own mother had begun. Daughter and mother-in-law usually developed a deep and continuing bond.

Have you ever imagined the mentoring that went on—woman to woman—in the Bible accounts? Think of Elizabeth, while pregnant with John (the Baptist), being the mentor to the young virgin Mary, who was awaiting the birth of the Messiah she carried in her womb.

Naomi repeatedly referred to her daughter-in-law Ruth as "my daughter," and we know she taught her about spiritual things. Ruth would not leave her when Naomi decided as a widow to return to her people. "Your people will be my people and your God my God," Ruth told her (see Ru 1:16b).

Lois, a woman in the New Testament, instilled spiritual truths into her daughter Eunice, who had a son named Timothy. Together grandmother and mother had an impact on this young evangelist whom Paul highly treasured as one who would later carry on his ministry.

Dorcas, a well-known seamstress, was resurrected after her death because she was so needed. Ever thought of all the others she might have taught to sew?

WHAT CAN I DO?

You are responsible to God only for sharing what you have, but what blessing comes from teaching what you have learned to the younger—or even the "younger in the Lord."

Citing Paul's words to Titus, about the older women teaching the younger, Liz discipled several younger housewives to teach them efficient housekeeping techniques. But their real purpose in cleaning homes in their community was to pray as they dusted. Thus these housekeepers called themselves "The Houseblessers."

When Liz shared her vision for blessing homes, Laura immediately remembered some of the most sage advice she had ever received. It was shortly before she and Brooks were married, and Mrs. J.O. Williams was teaching a seminar on "Love, Courtship and Marriage." She said, "Never pick up anything twice, whether it is a pair of socks or a quarrel." Practical, and spiritual, like the ministry of these houseblessers.

As the only "older" women in a young women's Bible study, Jan—the teacher—and Lois take seriously their responsibility to lead the younger women.

Because of the uniqueness of their church which draws many people from dysfunctional homes, it soon became apparent that some of the girls lacked basic homemaking skills which they would have learned naturally in a "normal" family setting.

Rather than trying to teach the class about entertaining in a dry classroom setting, Jan and Lois hosted a morning tea in Lois' home, making learning interesting and fun.

As they enjoyed scones and jam with their tea, questions were asked about the table setting, recipes, various napkin folds, care of linens, and use of silverware.

"Oops! I spilled some cream on this lovely tablecloth!" one of the young women exclaimed.

"No problem. I have just the thing," Lois assured her. As the spot disappeared, Lois made use of an opportunity to extol the virtues of a certain stain-removing product and an opening to discuss other ways to keep nice things nice.

The goal was to instill in these young wives the assurance that each one could be confident entertaining in her own home, with whatever she had on hand, even mixed-pattern dishes and utensils as Lois did. She stressed the importance of expressing their God-given uniqueness as hostesses.

Older women sometimes feel threatened by the younger generation; the younger feel intimidated by the older. But if there is a skill you want to learn, find a more accomplished person—whatever her chronological age or marital status—and ask her to teach you that skill. Nothing is more flattering to a gifted person than for someone to share her interest. Single women can mentor married women and vice versa. The important thing is to learn from one another, then to share what you have learned with others, to pass on the skills and knowledge.

Quoting Paul again: "Do nothing out of selfish ambition or vain conceit, but in humility consider others better than yourselves. Each of you should look not only to your own interests, but also to the interests of others" (Phil 2:3-4).

Find a gracious Christian woman blessed in the skills you need. Ask her, "Will you 'Titus' me?" If she is in tune with the Holy Spirit, she will find time and ways to help.

Then look around you. There may be dozens of young women who need *your* homemaking skills. Share them.

15

The Proverbs 31 Principle

In the house of the wise are stores of choice food and oil, but a foolish man devours all he has. **Proverbs 21:20**

DRAGGING OUT OF BED at 6:45 A.M., exhausted from coughing much of the night, I stumbled into the kitchen. The family were already sitting around the table waiting for me so LeRoy could read the morning Scripture. Just as he began, our youngest jumped up, ran to the refrigerator, grabbed a half gallon of orange juice and dripped it across the new kitchen rug.

"Don't you have any reverence for God's Word?" I scolded more angry about the orange juice spill than the fact that she interrupted our family devotions.

"Sit down and listen," I ordered, picking up a towel to soak up the spilled juice.

By now none of us wanted to hear the Bible reading. My reaction had ruined the start of our new day. Though I asked the family and the Lord to forgive me, I couldn't wipe the incident from my mind.

As I dropped clothes into the washer later that morning, I prayed, "Lord, I'm ready to throw in my dish towel. Why can't I be like the truly good woman described in Proverbs 31?"

Deep in my heart it seemed he said, "The virtuous woman did not get that way overnight. Neither will you. Her good qualities were developed over a period of time. Let me help you."

I was impressed and stretched when I saw the way *The Living Bible* states this high standard for a woman:

She finds wool and flax and busily spins it. She buys imported foods, brought by ship from distant ports. She gets up before dawn to prepare breakfast for her household, and plans the day's work for her servant girls. She goes out to inspect a field, and buys it; with her own hands she plants a vineyard. She is energetic, a hard worker, and watches for bargains. She works far into the night.

She sews for the poor, and generously gives to the needy. She has no fear of winter for her household, for she has made warm clothes for all of them. She upholsters with finest tapestry; her own clothing is beautifully made—a purple gown of pure linen.... She makes belted linen garments to sell to the merchants.

She is a woman of strength and dignity, and has no fear of old age. When she speaks, her words are wise, and kindness is the rule of everything she says. She watches carefully all that goes on throughout her household, and is never lazy. Her children stand and bless her; so does her husband.... Charm can be deceptive and beauty doesn't last, but a woman who fears and reverences God shall be greatly praised.

Proverbs 31:13-22, 24-28, 30 TLB

WHAT IS A HOMEMAKER?

Barbara Bush has said, "Our country's future is in our house." Note that the Proverbs 31 woman's "children stand and bless her; so does her husband." In other words, she is a homemaker:

She is a person who makes a home. To her a home must be more than a motel and fast-food stop. Just as she recognizes that the family is the strength of a nation, she knows that the home is the strength of the family. She strives to make her home a place of beauty, order, and security—a positive retreat from a negative and turbulent world. There her family finds the healing and refreshing they need to face the world anew each day. There they are built up, rather than beaten down. There they can be open and vulnerable, knowing they are loved unconditionally.

That is the home this homemaker strives to create, realizing that she has the important role of mood-setter and atmosphere-maker for her home.[1]

Traditionally, a homemaker is assumed to be a married woman who stays at home, raising the children. But today a homemaker can be anyone who creates a home where others are welcomed, loved, and refreshed. Whether male or female, single or married, we are called to make a dwelling place our "home."

NO FEAR OF THE FUTURE

The Proverbs 31 woman had no fear of the future—only a reverential fear of the Lord.

My theory is two-fold: I believe while she trusted the Lord, she was also prepared. She planned ahead for winter and for any other unexpected dilemma her family might face.

Matthew Henry, writing in 1710, comments on the Proverbs 31 woman stocking up for the days ahead:

> In verse 5 she lays up for hereafter; she shall rejoice in time to come, having laid in a good stock for her family, and having good portions for her children.[2]

When America's economy was primarily agricultural, a home-maker filled her cellar with home-canned fruits and vegetables in the summer, in preparation for winter. She did not hoard—but stored. Many homes also had storm cellars for the family's protection. I like the way the New International Version translates verse 25b: "She can laugh at the days to come," because she is prepared.

Several years ago the elders in Peter Lord's church distributed a memo concerning the future. They felt God was giving us definite signs of coming events so we could be prepared. Among their suggestions:

1. The development of strong relationships, especially with our Christian brothers and sisters.
2. Getting out of debt.
3. A simpler lifestyle with a proper diet to maintain good health.
4. A food supply for the family.
5. Sharpening our skills to do things ourselves, for ourselves and others.

Because storm clouds are hanging low over the future, there is no reason to excuse preparation in any way for the future. We ought to be diligent in the preparation of ourselves: body, soul, and spirit. Rejoice, lift up your heads. Your redemption draweth nigh. And till then, if it gets darker, we rejoice for we are in the Light business; if all around seems dreary, rejoice for we are in the Life business; and if hate is everywhere, we are in the Love business.[3]

THE MODERN HOMEMAKER

While many of us do not grow our own vegetables nor do we can or freeze large supplies of vegetables, there are precautions we can take for potential emergencies.

A smart idea is to pack a suitcase with needed supplies, rotating the items from time to time so they stay fresh. The supplies needed depend on whether you live in an area prone to tornados, earthquakes, hurricanes, snow and ice storms, floods or other climatic unpredictables. After many evacuations from hurricane threats to the Florida coastlines, I suggest when the Lord warns you, obey his instructions. Sometimes he will tell you well in advance: "Get ready, now!"

We can keep our home pantry stocked with items easy to prepare even without electricity—canned goods, peanut butter, crackers, nuts, powdered milk, bottled water. Not hoarded—stored.

A bonus: by having extra food on hand, we can easily take care of any unexpected company. Who of us hasn't been caught unprepared when out-of-town friends stopped in unannounced? Feeding them is extending hospitality.

In your canvas EMERGENCY EVACUATION KIT pack: a Bible, bottled water, powdered fruit drink mixes and/or powdered milk, a portable radio, adequate batteries, a flashlight, first aid kit, extra prescription medicines, toilet articles including soap, washcloth, towel, toothbrushes and toothpaste, non-perishable foods, cups and eating utensils, can opener, matches and candles, a blanket, umbrella, good walking shoes, large garbage sacks, toilet paper, a bedsheet or two (good also for a tablecloth or making bandages), disinfectants, change of underwear, a sewing kit.[4]

Keep extra cash on hand. Once we saw long lines of people waiting at an automatic bank to get money, delaying their hurricane evacuation to a danger point.

Include children's toys, games, books to amuse them. Even

adults enjoy these games if housed in an emergency shelter for several days.

Water purification pills are vital when the water supply is contaminated.

Plan in advance an emergency "contact point" where you can call or meet the family members you might get separated from.

Keep warm coats and rain apparel handy where you can grab one for each member of the family if you must evacuate. Coats are good substitutes for blankets for overnight in a shelter or a car.

Keep some items for emergencies in your purse, such as aspirin, a small sewing kit, bandaids, and a flashlight. I once was caught in Argentina in a twelve-hour electrical shutoff at night, and the hotel did not have enough candles for guests. When I had twelve flights of stairs to climb in a hotel in a country where I did not speak their language, I wished for the flashlight I'd left in my suitcase upstairs!

Keep calm. Do not fear. Take cover if a tornado is approaching. Leave for higher ground as soon as you receive the word for a hurricane evacuation. (Don't try to sit it out.)

HER HUSBAND BLESSES HER

Another aspect of Proverbs 31:28 strikes me as particularly relevant to our subject of hospitality for the Christian woman: "So does her husband" (stand up and bless her). Why? Look at verse 23 in the New International Version: "Her husband is respected at the city gate, where he takes his seat among the elders of the land."

The Proverbs 31 homemaker respects her husband and supports him however she can.

Laura and Brooks have a story about that principle.

One of the turning points in their five-year-old church's organization came when the men began to meet each week to pray for direction. It was also a blessing to Brooks and Laura's marriage when she agreed to host the meeting in their home.

They had moved around so much their furniture was getting shabby. So to prepare for the meetings, Brooks bought some new chairs—which blessed Laura! And Laura baked special cakes or pies each week to give the meeting a relaxed, welcoming atmosphere.

The men loved it! They met at the Watsons' regularly for a couple of years; out of that was formulated a church structure of elders that continues—with modification—to this day, almost twenty years later.

"KEEPERS AT HOME"

Seven years ago Denise Boggs came up with a novel idea that blossomed into a business she calls "Keepers at Home Creations." Wanting to minister to the spiritual, emotional, and financial needs of women who desire to earn some income while staying at home with their children, Denise explained the goals she worked out.

> "Keepers at Home" work willingly with our hands to produce beautiful gift items that are marketed in a national chain of gift shops as well as retail outlets.... Spiritual needs are met through a weekly Bible study and prayer time. Emotional needs are met through interaction with other women with small children and the encouragement of praying for one another's needs. Financial needs are met under the leadership of a director who trains the women to design and assemble gift items.
>
> Our Keepers at Home group is learning to barter. Bartering is to be a type of refuge and answer to the time the Bible describes when we won't be able to buy or sell. If that time does not take us by surprise, then we won't be caught unaware and panic.

When they meet each week, following the teaching and prayer, they have a bartering session: "This is what I have..." and "This is what I need..." One may need a haircut or permanent—she can exchange a lovely silk flower arrangement for it. Another has garden vegetables to trade for a blue blouse.[5]

THE TRULY HAPPY HOMEMAKER

All these principles exemplified by the Proverbs 31 woman are summed up by Baukje Doornenbal in *Homemaking*:

A happy homemaker, convinced of her importance as an individual and a contributor to the lives of those around her, forms the backbone of the family. And in turn, good families constitute the building blocks of society. Women in the home, therefore, can exert a crucial influence on their society.[6]

Women, whether married or single, have a critical role in society, because of the significance in welcoming, nurturing, encouraging, and caring for others. These principles, when implemented, have a critical impact in the world.

16

Reciprocal Living

God has given each of you some special abilities; be sure to use them to help each other, passing on to others God's many kinds of blessings. **1 Peter 4:10 TLB**

"WE'VE GOT A FELLOWSHIP CRISIS in the church at large," Mary Jo commented as we sat in her living room recently. This woman who has spent many years teaching Christians concluded: "We're too self-centered."

Unfortunately, that is often too true. Instead of love and unity among believers, frequently we see rivalry, division, indifference. How far we have come from the first-century church which concerned itself with "reciprocal living" based on commands for "one another living."

The phrases "one another" and "each other" are reciprocal pronouns. Reciprocal living for Christians refers then to the mutual obligations and relationships we have as a result of our common relationship with Christ as members of his body.

There are over fifty "one anothers" in the New Testament. Let's look at a few of them:

- Pray for one another: "Therefore confess your sins to each other and pray for each other so that you may be healed. The prayer of a righteous man is powerful and effective." (Jas 5:16)
- Love one another: "A new command I give you: Love one another. As I have loved you, so you must love one another." (Jn 13:34)
- Receive one another: "Accept one another, then, just as Christ accepted you, in order to bring praise to God." (Rom 15:7)
- Use hospitality to one another: "Each one should use whatever gift he has received to serve others, faithfully administering God's grace in its various forms." (1 Pt 4:10)

NEW TESTAMENT EXAMPLES

In the early church there was a mixture of races, religious backgrounds, and social classes—Jews, barbarians, Greeks, slaves, free men, rich, poor. Jews sometimes looked down on Gentile brothers, and vice versa. Paul had to tell them, "... receive ye one another, even as Christ also received us, to the glory of God" (Rom 15:7 KJV).

Scripture commands and the Holy Spirit commissions every believer to be concerned about caring for one another.

Some of the more obscure examples of hospitality, easy to overlook in the New Testament, have the most to teach us about hospitality. You will find these stories in the Scripture passages referenced.

- Phoebe: Paul instructed the believers in Rome to care for the needs of Phoebe "in a way worthy of the saints" because this visiting Christian sister had been a helper of many, including Paul. (See Rom 16:1-2)

- Philemon: He must have been a cordial host, because Paul felt free to invite himself to stay with him. (See Phlm 22)
- Simon the tanner provided Peter with lodging and food while in Joppa, meaning Simon's home became Peter's while he was there ministering. (See Acts 10:5-6; 10:10)
- Gaius was commended by Paul for allowing him and the whole church in Corinth to enjoy his hospitality. (See Rom 16:23)
- Philip, one of the original seven deacons and an evangelist, opened his Caesarea home to Paul and Luke while they were in the vicinity. (See Acts 21:8)
- Cornelius, a Roman centurion, had a vision and sent for Peter to come to inform him about the ways of Jesus. He believed, along with his relatives and close friends, and the Holy Spirit was poured out on Gentiles for the first time. (See Acts 10:9-48)
- Paul's Philippian jailer, on the verge of suicide when a violent earthquake caused prison doors to come free so prisoners could escape, was instead persuaded by Paul to believe in Jesus and receive eternal life—along with his whole household. The jailer brought Paul and Silas to his home for a meal. (see Acts 16:27-34)
- Mnason of Cyrus provided lodging for Paul, Luke, and some of the disciples from Caesarea as they neared Jerusalem. This may well have meant opening his home to Gentile believers as well as Jews, which would have taken courage in the light of that time's persecution. (See Acts 21:16)

We need to remember that every member of the body of Christ has a unique God-given ability and ministry which is essential for the upbuilding of the others. The purpose of reciprocal living is that believers enable one another in Christian living and thus demonstrate together the love and unity that should characterize God's people.

In reading Acts 2:42-47, we see the development of community, indicating a continuous pattern in the Jerusalem church. There was a commitment to Scripture, to one another, to prayer, to praise, to worship, and to outreach. We see no fellowship crisis.

One pastor, contrasting the early church with the twentieth-century church in America, said that in the first years following Pentecost, believers ate, worked, prayed, and enjoyed fellowship together in their homes on a regular basis, not just two hours on Sunday morning. Because they helped each other, all their needs were met.

MEANINGFUL RELATIONSHIPS

A church with an effective outreach explains their motto:

We say we are "a people built together into a meaningful relationship in Christ."... It means we are a servant people, freely loving and caring for one another based on the grace we each experienced through Jesus. It does not mean that we belong to a club, organization, or activity, but rather to Christ and to each other.... We strive to be totally committed and totally involved. To expect less is to play church rather than to be the Church.[1]

LeRoy witnessed an example of this kind of one-anothering last spring. For a long time he had been flipping pancakes for numbers of young people who packed our apartment after late Sunday afternoon chapel on our Bible school campus. Then, when he had to have knee replacement surgery, those are the ones, from our extended family, who took turns driving him across Dallas to physical therapy three times a week for a couple of months. Some rearranged work and school schedules. One-anothering: caring for each other, bearing one another's burdens, being hospitable to one another.

HOW CAN I HELP OTHERS?

"Would you put an 'open for business' sign on your heart today?" author Jerry Cook challenged our congregation. "Don't get numb to other people's pain," he warned.

For weeks I could not escape his words. How could I have an open heart?

God soon answered my question by showing me a man sitting on the curb right in front of me.

"Just a poor homeless man," I thought to myself (eyeing him as I went into the bank where I cashed a check.

"Give him some money," the Lord seemed to say.

"But, Lord, there are so many like him out in the streets...."

"Do it for me!"

By the time I reached the man he was sitting there eating a hamburger, his sign asking for work propped up against him.

"The Lord Jesus wants you to have this," I said, pushing a few bills into his hand.

"Well, isn't that just like our wonderful Jesus? I only met him for the first time last week. He has been so kind to me. See this hamburger? A lady just brought it to me from McDonald's. Won't you sit down and share it with me?"

I smiled. A homeless, hungry man, offering me a part of his hamburger—maybe the only meal he has had today. A brand new believer.

"Thank you very much, but no thanks. I have lunch waiting at home," I told him. Back in the car I thanked the Lord that he had allowed me to meet one so recently born into his kingdom. One with no teaching, yet already he was demonstrating reciprocal living—sharing with one another.

Jesus said the poor we would always have with us. In *Daily Life in the Time of Jesus* we are told:

One of the most usual actions in the life of a Jew was to give money or a piece of bread to the unfortunate who begged for it in the street.... Beggars wandered along the roads, going to the markets and the fords of the river, and profiting too by the permission the Law gave them to eat ears of corn in the fields and grapes in the vineyards, providing they carried neither basket nor sickle, and to pick up windfalls and gather overlooked bunches.[2]

Thus they made ongoing provision for the hungry. But how can we help today?

HOW SOME HELP

When we attended the congregation where members registered their God-given gifts at the church office, volunteering to help one another, my gift was to teach writing classes; LeRoy's was to help the young men in the church repair their cars on Saturdays in our side yard.

Then we moved across the state to be close to my mother where I became the primary caregiver when she was fighting cancer throughout the last thirteen months of her life. How I needed help! But no longer were we in a church where I could call the secretary and ask, "Have you any nursing skills registered? Someone I could call to help me?"

Now some ten years later that same church has found the vision for helping one another. They are enlisting men and women with compassionate hearts and practical gifts, to serve and support those who are homebound with disability due to age or sickness and are unable to participate in activities of daily living.

Traveling around the country I have observed a number of ways certain people have learned to help. Here are a few:

- Kathy, Laura's daughter, saw the need for her parents to have a few days' respite from caring for Laura's mother, an Alzheimer's victim. When they came to Kathy's house in Alabama for Christmas, Kathy sent Laura and Brooks to a motel for a few days while she kept her grandmother in her own home. "What a blessing," Laura says. "We were worn out, emotionally and physically."

- Liz can't clean her flower beds because she is highly allergic to wasp stings (once she almost died). So the women in her small home group come regularly to weed Liz's flower beds.
- On the first Sunday of each month, a church in Florida collects donated foods and paper products to be distributed by their "Matthew 25:35 Food Ministry" to the needy in their community. The church has built a separate building to house this supply.
- Darlene keeps Sara's children one morning a week so Sara can visit in the home for the elderly. Shy Darlene thinks tending to children is more her gift than cheering up strangers in a nursing home.
- Bab cleans house for other women on Tuesdays. Cleaning house is what she enjoys doing, and she does this ministry as unto the Lord.
- Elizabeth and Mary, both gifted in arranging flowers, surprise their friends often with fresh or dried arrangements they have made. They also conduct classes—free of charge— to teach others how to do this.

PRAY FOR ONE ANOTHER

Each of us has at least one gift we can offer God by using it to serve the body of Christ. One of the greatest exchanges we can do is to pray for one another. We read accounts of early believers praying both in the temple and in homes.

Remember the story of Peter and John en route to pray in the temple at three in the afternoon—at the appointed time of prayer. They were serious about praying. Just before entering the temple that day, they healed a man crippled from birth. "Then Peter said, 'Silver or gold I do not have, but what I have

I give you. In the name of Jesus Christ of Nazareth, walk'"
(Acts 3:6).

The first Christians met primarily in homes, ideal places to
meet for prayer. Peter was miraculously freed from prison by an
angel, while a group of believers met at the home of John
Mark's mother, Mary. So involved in prayer, they had a hard
time believing it was actually Peter at the gate knocking—the
answer to prayer actually standing at their door.

Because the early church was under much persecution, they
knew how to pray with fervency. The Apostle James instructed
them about prayer:

> Is any one of you in trouble? He should pray. Is anyone
> happy? Let him sing songs of praise. Is any one of you sick?
> He should call the elders of the church to pray over him and
> anoint him with oil in the name of the Lord. And the prayer
> offered in faith will make the sick person well; the Lord will
> raise him up. If he has sinned, he will be forgiven. Therefore
> confess your sins to each other and pray for each other so
> that you may be healed. The prayer of a righteous man is
> powerful and effective.   James 5:13-16

Persistent prayer—praying without ceasing. Something we
are all commissioned to do.

HELPING WHEN SOMEONE DIES

At these times we're often at a loss for what to say to the person who is grieving. The best course here is to just be natural.

When Laura's daddy died, a friend of her mother's, Sara, simply held Laura's hand tight. That, with the look of compassion
in her eyes, spoke volumes.

Just don't be superficial like the lady who used to pat me on
the back every Sunday at church when I was the primary care-

giver for my dying mother. "I am sure you are walking in victory, Quin, knowing where your mother is going to spend eternity. Keep the upper lip stiff." I wanted to turn and run when I saw her crossing the church parking lot headed my way.

But don't be afraid to talk about the one who has died. Otherwise it would seem as though his life was inconsequential. Jackie says, "I *like* to talk about Jamie. He's still part of me." In fact, whenever their home group is together, it seems Jamie's name always comes into the conversation, quoting something profound or maybe something silly—he always seemed to have had *something* to say about almost any topic.

Write notes of encouragement. After the funeral is over, the relatives have left, and you are sitting among the belongings of your loved one trying to decide what to discard, tears roll down your cheeks. Now is when it is good to get a note in the mail or a short phone call of encouragement.

Offer practical help. Susan Jones once helped me take Mother to the hospital fifty miles from home. And within minutes after Mother died at home, Susan came to vacuum her room and help me get the smell of cancer and death out of it.

LOVING HELP = RECIPROCAL LIVING

Jamie said during his last illness, as his strength was waning, that the only guidance God was giving him was, "Don't do anything someone else can do." That is a good word at any time for all of us—operate in our own gifts, not worrying about someone else's gifts.

We are free to carry God's message in the way he has gifted each of us, expanding Jesus' work by proclaiming and extending God's word to the sphere of influence each of us has—not overlapping, not holding back to "let George do it," but boldly moving forward as the Lord directs. For instance, Laura and I have used the writing techniques handed down to us from

Jamie (a master storyteller) in writing this book.

In one of his columns, commenting on a principle discovered by Catherine Marshall, Jamie wrote:

> In reading excerpts of Catherine's daily journal, a secret of living emerged: When all else has been experienced and felt, Catherine realized we must start loving without reservation and criticism and in return allow others to love us.
>
> This is the lesson of the sufferings of the cross. That we might love each other even as Christ loves us. Only in laying down our lives and sharing in His love can we find the true purpose of the resurrection.[3]

17

Commitment
to Community

May the Lord make your love increase and overflow for each other and for everyone else, just as ours does for you. 1 Thessalonians 3:12

HOME CHURCH, or home group, community is a fascinating art form.

Except for the clackety-clack-clack of castanets often accompanying it, many people know little about flamenco guitar music. It, like the home church concept, is a revolutionary art form. When Craig began to play flamenco, Laura learned that although it seems totally spontaneous, improvised around a basic theme, flamenco has very strict rules of rhythm and certain characteristic chord patterns. The guitarist never plays things quite the same way twice.

Like the flamenco rhythms, the Holy Spirit follows set patterns. While it is very apparent that the theme is love harmonized by forgiveness, the Spirit never orchestrates his melody of community relationship the same way twice. And, like flamenco, each group's demonstration appears totally spontaneous to those involved.

C.W. Brister, in *Pastoral Care in the Church*, says of small groups:

> One of the reasons why people attend a particular church is that they choose a faith community where they feel at home, in a group where they (1) experience acceptance and a sense of belonging; (2) get help through discipleship training; (3) develop their spiritual gifts; and (4) participate meaningfully in the church's life and work. Belonging is more essential than merely attending, both for the individual and for the common life of the entire church.[1]

The first Christians met primarily in homes—they did not have church buildings until the third century. However, the Jerusalem believers, having such a large group, met in Solomon's Colonnade (see Acts 5:12). Homes, then, were ideal places to meet for prayer.

The term "home church" may be revolutionary to some people, primarily because they have some misconceptions about it. But when you think about it, the church was never just a building. The church was always intended to be the people who follow Jesus. So the church is the people who meet in a building. Whether they come together in a magnificent cathedral in an ancient city or in the basement of a humble home in some obscure village in a Third World country, wherever believers meet is church.

For several years now we have had a growing excitement about "home churches." It is as though a drummer keeps beating time with a message: "Get ready. Get ready. Get your homes ready."

We believe God is preparing hundreds of homes for believers to worship in, and he is going to need more. As time accelerates into the last of the last days, it is in the small group setting where we can really get down to the business of living out our Christian life as the early Christians did. What better place can we go for this kind of rich experience than into our homes?

Leith Anderson, in *A Church for the 21st Century*, focuses on the critical need that is met by this type of ministry:

> As families have either fractured or taken on different forms, they function less as small groups.... Consequently, the church is increasingly composed of individuals rather than families.... Many of these people who have felt this social fragmentation have found that support groups provide lasting relationships, escape from loneliness, and opportunity to address and resolve their personal problems.[2]

NEW TESTAMENT COMMUNITY

God showed us patterns for this kind of ministry in several New Testament settings.

Soon after Paul and Silas were released from prison, they went to the home of Lydia, a prominent businesswoman who had been Paul's first European convert to Christianity. Her home in Philippi was the scene of many prayer meetings with Paul himself serving as teacher at times.

Aquila and Priscilla, a dedicated husband-wife team, held "church" in their homes in Ephesus, Corinth, and Rome. Since they were both tentmakers, their home in the weaving sections of Corinth and Ephesus became a rendezvous for those wanting to know more about the Christian faith. In fact, Paul even made his home with them for a while in Corinth. Since they were such a hospitable couple, it is likely they invited the eloquent Apollos to stay with them while they "expounded unto him the way of

God more perfectly" (Acts 18:26 KJV).

Our own experiences follow these rhythms and patterns in a remarkable way.

COSTLY DISCIPLESHIP

We began a small home meeting at the Watsons' home. While we were praying we heard a funny noise—someone was "egging" the front door. Brooks had just that day hung a new door. It had not even been stained yet. Now it was messed up with egg dribbling down it. As often happens when we upset Satan by beginning a work in tune with the Lord, the devil was trying to steal our joy.

We took this as a sign that we were in God's will. Instead of staining the door, Brooks simply painted it. As long as the Watsons lived in that house, the door remained egg-yolk yellow—a cheerful reminder that whenever we are shunned for Jesus' sake, he will give us grace to rejoice in the midst of it.

That was such a special group that began meeting that night. Soon two single women and another couple were added to our number. For two years this group of ten got together on Saturday nights. We ate supper in each others' homes and just visited or studied our Bibles or prayed for one another's needs.

It was a fellowship meeting, nothing heavy, just getting to know each other. We found that when we rubbed shoulders regularly, the chips fell off fast.

In that home group we really did not know one another, until we committed our lives to one another on a spiritual basis. Knowing we were brothers and sisters in the Lord, we first learned to accept each other "as is." As we recognized Jesus in the lives around us, that acceptance generated admiration, admiration sparked respect, and respect grew into love. We had become more than close friends—we were close relatives in the household of God.

Then, when two years had passed, God sent us out into various aspects of ministry—and after a number of years each one is still working in the kingdom of God in a place of leadership. No wonder the devil got riled up on our first meeting!

AN ALL-AGE GROUP

One couple (Frank and Linda) launched a home church keyed to young families. They included several single mothers—which meant children were involved. They found the mothers who wanted their children with them were usually the very ones who did not know how to handle them.

Thus Linda developed a program for the children, who met downstairs while the adults were in the upstairs family room. Often one of the Howards' teenagers or another young person met with the kids. They kept the program short, sometimes using an appropriate videotape, followed by a fun time. Actually, when they drew pictures and wrote letters to missionaries, the children considered this part of their fun time!

Meeting in a family setting with other adults (married and single), and the children taken care of, freed the adults to concentrate on their own worship and Bible study. They prayed for each other but had no in-depth counseling within the group until refreshment time. At nine o'clock sharp the announcement, "We need to go downstairs for refreshments now," meant those who needed to get school-age children home could leave early. They did not discourage in-depth ministry during group time, but Frank let it be known that if someone had a special need, he would stay upstairs with them for counseling and prayer.

Linda says, "We found that adhering to a set schedule was our key to success. We were not only committed to the nine p.m. cut-off time, Frank and I were committed to being there every Tuesday evening. We gave the house key to one of the group so they could still meet even when we were on vacation."

STRUCTURED GROUP

LeRoy and I went deeper into reciprocal living when we entered into a home church relationship a bit more disciplined in structure and aims than Frank and Linda's group.

After church services on Sunday night, sixteen adults met at our house to be taught by our pastor. We wanted to know one another at a deeper level, becoming transparent, honest, and open with one another. It is not always easy sharing your life with someone else when you are shy by nature!

We began our meetings with songs of praise, led by two guitarists. The rest of us made a joyful noise unto the Lord on simple rhythm band instruments—tambourines, cymbals, triangles, maracas, and sticks. Sometimes we would sing choruses from the Bible; other times we chose old-time gospel favorites.

The main emphasis of the evening was sharing what we learned in a homework assignment we worked on during the week. We spent several months exploring reciprocal commands in the Bible. What did God mean when he said to have the same care for one another? How can we do it? How can I serve my sister in Christ this week, or the new mother sitting across the table from me who looks so tired?

We learned, particularly, to love each other in spite of our weaknesses and differences of opinion. The hardest was to expose ourselves—that true self below the tip of the iceberg— where few people ever see.

The pastor and his wife, Johnnie, led us to adopt a set of guidelines to help us develop our Christian walk on a daily basis. It was through these disciplines that I really learned hospitality—often *pushed* beyond what I would have done to welcome people into my home.

We agreed:

- to spend at least 30 minutes a day communicating with the Lord in a quiet time.
- to pray with our spouse at least three times a week
- to spend at least one hour a week in intercessory prayer

- to spend time with our children each day
- to fast one meal a week and one full day a month
- to exercise our bodies ten minutes each day
- to tithe our income
- to operate our home on a budget based on Bible principles
- to keep in touch with our parents by letter or phone regularly
- to entertain for Christ's sake in our home at least once a month
- to pray regularly for each couple in our group as well as their children
- to pray for our governmental leaders and write them letters of encouragement
- to do our Bible homework assignment each week, studying the Word and writing out how it can be applied in our everyday life

MIDWEEK GROUP

LeRoy and I also hosted a midweek home church with a similar format. But we had some who were married to non-believers, so this was not a couples group in the same way as the Sunday night home church, nor were the disciplines the same.

The Wednesday night group supported a prison ministry. Several of the men went to a nearby state prison on Thursday night to conduct church services for the more than thirty prisoners who had become Christians during their incarceration. The Wednesday group "covered" these teachers and the prison church with prayer.

They also corresponded with some of the prisoners and sent them Bibles, Christian books, and toiletries or shoes, which the prisoners must officially request. At Christmas the women in the group baked goodies for the chapel services closest to Christmas Day.

This, too, is hospitality. Jesus said, "I was in prison and ye came unto me" (Mt 25:36b KJV).

FOCUSED PRAYER GROUPS

I was once in a focused prayer group that started sponta-
neously because six mothers were concerned about our children. Every Monday morning—for three long years—we met at
Fran Ewing's home at five *a.m.* for an hour of prayer. We witnessed numerous answers to prayers, including miraculous turn-
arounds in most of our youngsters. My three children were
among those.

Some home prayer groups meet for general prayer purposes,
for their own needs, for their city, neighborhood, or friends.
But some of my most fruitful prayer meetings have been when
we gathered in homes for focused prayer.

One root word for "intercessor" or "intercession" is paga
(sometimes spelled pagah), meaning "to come between, to
assail, to cause to entreat."[3] When an Israeli soldier hits the
mark in target practice, he shouts "Paga!"—the modern
Hebrew equivalent of "Bull's eye!" Effective intercessors learn
to "hit the bull's eye" in prayer.

Recently LeRoy and I sat with twenty-eight parents on Bob
and Dottie Sims' spacious patio in Lexington, Kentucky for
focused prayer. After studying my book, *How to Pray for Your
Children*, these parents have met weekly for three years to pray
for one another's children.

After a covered dish meal and fellowship, they gather in a circle to share how God has answered their prayers. As dark
approaches, they divide into smaller groups, scattering into different parts of the yard and house to pray for children—not
their own, but for another parent's child. They continue to pray
for that child until the next week when they get the name and
need of another child to pray for all week.

Started by Elizabeth and Harry Stuart, there are now several
home prayer groups in Kentucky who have the profound purpose of praying for their children—from infants to adults. The
enthusiasm and interest of the fathers to pray for their children
thrilled me.

COVENANT RELATIONSHIPS

Someone has pointed out that Jesus operated on the principle of "hungering and thirsting." He asked the woman at the well for water. Her hunger drew out the life that was in him—both physical and spiritual food.

Because of their ongoing hunger and thirst for this kind of life, Laura and Brooks have been in a group that has met every week for fifteen years. This group of six couples decided to enter into "covenant relationship." At the beginning they covenanted together to pray for each other daily—which they have continued to do—and to keep all conversation within the group confidential—also a continuing factor. So their covenant commitment was one where they agreed to walk together in love and trust.

The group's format has been to go around the room letting each person "check in" each Monday night. They share their deep needs and victories, spiritual or practical—and sometimes find the practical is quite spiritual. Coordinating the group is a businessman, a born manager, who keeps everyone on the subject, not letting anyone dominate the conversation—though some may have more to share than others on any given evening. All in this group are in places of leadership in their church, but this is a place where they can bring their personal needs quite apart from their church business, to air them and receive direction, correction, and affirmation. Laura and Brooks' group does a lot of talking, but they also do a lot of listening, to each other and to the Lord.

PRIORITIES

One night the discussion centered—as it often does—on how committed they are to the priorities God has shown them for day-to-day living. While talk swirled around her, Laura scribbled down fast a list of questions that were being asked:

What has God given me?
What am I to do with it?
Why am I not moving ahead?
What does God want?
Why am I not getting it?
Why is God not getting it?
Where am I bound?
Why am I bound?
How do I get free?
When free, what do I do?
Am I afraid?
What is the price?
Do I want to pay it?
Do I want to give up what I've got to get it?

In the beginning only two questions—the first and the last—were settled in her heart. She knew God had given her certain talents, and she knew he wanted her to use them in a new way.

The other answers were not so obvious. But as she went about her daily routine, she found clues popping up in unexpected places—while reading a catalog or in conversation with a stranger—as well as in the expected ones—while reading her Bible or listening to a sermon. One by one the answers came. And she is learning a lot about her own actions and reactions in the process.

CREATIVE VACATIONS

Laura and Brooks' group has taken a number of vacations together. One of the couples has a rustic house in the mountains which their family built with their own hands. At first the group went with some fear and trepidation—after all, cooped up together in a small mountain cottage for a week! But it became a time of bonding, the highlight of their relationships. Each morning they have a quiet time, going off alone with

Bible and notepad. Then they come back together and share what God has impressed on them. They have learned how to relax creatively together.

OUTREACH

In order to prevent becoming ingrown, this group has continually sought outreach projects. They helped a missionary in Indonesia pay for getting electricity to his house. They help a ministry for rehabilitating street people. One year they redecorated the church's prayer room.

The pastor, Jamie Buckingham, was in this group. Though Jamie died in February 1992, his wife, Jackie, remains a very vital part of the group. After all, this is family. "So it was natural, since Jamie had taught us for so long how to live, then how to die, that now Jackie would teach us how to live victoriously as a widow," Laura says, a tear in her eye but a smile on her face.

COVENANT RELATIONSHIPS

In the beginning this group agreed to twelve reminders for covenant relationships:

1. Be personal, not abstract. In sharing, we do not deal with theological abstractions but with attitudes and feelings.
2. Intellectual opinions play no part in our discussions, except as they may bear upon our own personal lives.
3. Pray for one another daily. This is essential.
4. Try to set aside daily quiet time, involving reading, meditation, and prayer.
5. Confess no one's deficiencies but our own.
6. What is said in the group stays in the group.
7. No church business except as it affects us personally.
8. Pray immediately as the request comes up.

9. Be open and honest in statements and feelings.
10. Practice more affirmation.
11. Practice routine forgiveness.
12. Allow the freedom to express our feelings without being judged.

We must be careful in this kind of group not to make developing relationships our goal. Kenneth Schmidt writes: "Our goal must be to respond to Christ's love by obeying His commands. Our commitment is not to community but to love the people we're with."[4]

Just so, reflecting Christ's love, acceptance, and forgiveness creates relationships. The purpose of relationships? Rick Joyner says it well: "All spiritual labor is for the purpose of Christ being formed in His people."[5]

ANOTHER FORMAT

Home churches do not have to be for couples only. Linda Lees likes to tell a love story relating to another of their church's home groups, one that majors on evangelism and outreach:

Recently, Sue, a woman from this group, met a woman she had never seen before on the beach. They talked of several things as they walked along the edge of the surf; Sue told Ann of the home group she attended. The lady seemed interested, so Sue invited her to come along. That evening God spoke to Ann's heart about having drifted from him. She renewed her commitment and was reestablished with the Lord.

Ann came to the group regularly and one evening brought her live-in boyfriend. It was a night of sharing around the room of what God was doing in each life. When it was Will's turn to speak, he tried but could not seem to get out more than a few words without choking back tears. Finally Ann intervened with her own story, and the sharing continued around the room.

Several people asked for prayer that evening. One by one they sat in a chair pulled out into the center of the room as the other group members gathered around to pray. When all their requests had been taken care of and the group was about to close, Will haltingly spoke up. "Can you pray for someone as unworthy as I?" he asked. He was lovingly placed in the "prayer chair" and led in a prayer of repentance and acceptance of Jesus as his Savior. A few weeks later the couple was married and continue to be faithful participants in the group. Two people brought into God's kingdom, through home group ministry.

While home groups have varied structures, we can see the common denominator is support—one of the reasons Jesus established the church. In the home group structure we find personified the principles of Acts 2:46: apostles' teaching, fellowship, breaking bread from house to house, and prayer.

Carl George says, in *Prepare Your Church for the Future*, "I'm convinced that the larger part of ministry needs to take place in a family-like atmosphere of a small group meeting in a home."[6]

The home church, then, is where we can show hospitality by providing a setting for giving and receiving personal ministry.

Listen! Can't you almost hear the pulsating phrasing of a Holy Spirit-inspired flamenco melody?

Home group... home church... community—by whatever name—is, like flamenco music, truly a fascinating art form.

18

Manners and Graciousness

So that there is no division or discord or lack of adaptation (of the parts of the body to each other), but the members all alike have a mutual interest in and care for one another.   1 Corinthians 12:25 AMP

WHAT ARE GOOD MANNERS? The dictionary says it is polite social behavior. Graciousness is characterized by showing kindness and compassion, being thoughtful of others.

Marcus, one of our extended family in Dallas, is a true Kentucky gentleman. He offered us this list to define a real man of God:

- A gentleman is committed to pursuing the character of God in his life.
- He sees and finds a need, then fills it without being asked.

He volunteers his services with a willing heart. (He holds an umbrella for a woman during a rainstorm, pulls back her chair for her at the table, opens the car door for her.)

- He should not be discouraged if his politeness as a gentleman is rejected by a woman who is not used to being treated honorably.
- He unconditionally accepts people, is kind and considerate of everyone.
- He is a good communicator and asks questions for accuracy in phone calls, letters, messages. He takes other people's feelings into account.
- He addresses people respectfully by proper names, makes eye contact in conversation—both talking and listening.
- He has a daily reading of the Word and prayer time. He is knowledgeable of the Proverbs that will help him lead a blameless ethical life.
- A gentleman knows who he is in Christ.
- A gentleman is a servant, and a servant is a leader. He takes the lead with sensitivity as his guide.

Should men be included in hospitality? By all means. As mentioned in our introduction, one of the qualifications for leadership for men in the early church included the ministry of hospitality. Some men, like David and Greg, love to cook. Some of the best restaurant chefs are men. Other ways they contribute are by greeting guests at the door, praying over the meal, cleaning up, even simply chatting with guests.

That is the essence of manners and graciousness—making your guests comfortable, anticipating their needs, serving them.

BIBLICAL CUSTOMS SET EXAMPLES

Being considerate of others seems to have been in God's plan from the beginning.

For instance, when Abraham encountered his three special guests—sent from God—he eagerly greeted them and offered hospitality. We read in Genesis 18 how Abraham:

—hurried to meet them;
—had water brought to wash their tired, dirty feet;
—offered them rest under his tree;
—invited them to stay and eat a meal.

Rushing into his tent, he told Sarah to make some bread while he picked a choice calf for his servant to prepare for their unexpected guests.

Abraham was offering hospitality in a typical Middle Eastern fashion, expressing good manners. Notice that the husband here directed the hospitality. It was a joint effort, however, as the most gracious hospitality always is.

The *Encyclopedia Judaic* has this to say about biblical hospitality:

The Bible is replete with examples of pious hospitality. As soon as Abraham saw the three men of Mamre "from afar," he hurried to invite them into his house, ministered to their physical comfort, and served them lavishly (Gn 18). Similarly Laban was eager to welcome Abraham's servant (Gn 24:28-32) while Rebekah attended to the comfort of his camels.... Manoah did not allow the angel to depart before he had partaken of his hospitality (Jgs 13:15).... David repaid a courtesy which Barzillai had extended to his men (2 Sm 17:27-29), with a courtesy to Barzillai's servant Kimham (2 Sm 19:32-40).[1]

In New Testament times, the guest was greeted with a blessing of peace, kissed, his feet washed, his head anointed with oil, given water to drink, and served a meal.

Any stranger entering a town at the time of Jesus was usually sure of being invited to someone's home for food and lodging. Because of the laws of hospitality, Jesus could send his disciples out knowing they would be cared for in homes.

Today we might call it good manners or cultural expectations.

Laura and I grew up in a generation where manners were drilled into us on a daily basis. But many in today's generation have not had that discipline.

The aesthetics are important. Early in our friendship, Laura reminded me of this principle when she brought me flowers for our lunch table. "Genesis 2:17 says that God made every tree in the Garden of Eden pleasant to look at and good for food. He gave us the ability to appreciate beauty as he gave us beauty to appreciate," she said.

Picture in your mind a bare table with silverware plunked down in the middle, plates and bowls of food in no particular pattern. Isn't it more pleasing to see order on the table? We can honor our family and friends by setting a pretty table. And God, too, is honored thereby.

All "manners" would fit this premise since "manners" means treating others with respect, making them comfortable in your presence.

Our American manners have been much maligned at home and abroad, where too often we confirm the charge of "ugly Americans." Let us consider how we can change that image.

GOOD AMERICAN MANNERS

Introductions. The etiquette books tell us when you are introducing a woman and a man, always mention the woman's name first, for you are introducing the man to the woman. When being introduced, a young man should stand. He remains standing until the women and older men have found seats or until all who wish to sit have been offered a chair.

That may sound archaic, but think about it—it is a matter of honoring women and elders. Graciousness never goes out of style. Acceptable manners are appreciated by everyone.

In introducing your friends, find a mutual point of contact if possible, so they can begin a conversation. Something like, "You two have something in common—both of you have small children." Or, "You are both from Oregon—small world!"

Telephone manners. It's helpful to identify yourself when you are calling: "May I please speak with Mary? This is Dot Burns from Birmingham calling."

Use wisdom in whether to identify yourself or not when answering your phone. One can just say, "Hello" or "Watsons' residence." Since we have moved to Dallas, we get so many wrong number calls, I am convinced our number once belonged to folks who ran some kind of shady business.

More and more companies that I telephone have a receptionist answer something like this: "Mercy Ships. How may I direct your call?"

"Keith Sherrer, please," I reply.

I must tell you I had the "call waiting" removed from our home telephone services. I do not like to spend my money for a long distance phone call and be interrupted several times as the one with whom I'm talking tells me, "Hold on a minute—I have another call coming in."

Being interrupted once or twice I can handle—but not more than three times during one conversation, putting me on "hold." When I am put on hold too many times, it signals to me that I am not that important, and it comes across as inconsiderate telephone manners. If I have called when someone is on another line, I would rather get a busy signal and call them back or be told outright that they are busy on another line, and I will understand and phone again later.

I've been told about a mother who is frantic to get ahold of her teenager who is home alone—and tying up the phone line. Okay, Mom, it's time to set some time limits on phone use. Good manners again, consideration of others.

Table manners.

- When going to the table, ladies sit first. Gentlemen, seat the lady on your right if you are in a group. Then yourself.
- Napkin: After prayer, the napkin is placed on the lap entirely open if it is lunch-size, or in half if it is a dinner napkin. Guests wait until the hostess has taken up hers before placing their own. At banquets, as soon as you sit down place the napkin on your lap.
- Who is served first? Ladies usually, but the hostess is not served first unless she is the only lady at the table.
- If the hostess is serving you, you will be served from the left and plates are to be removed from your right.
- Table setting: In using the utensils at your plate, the usual rule is to start from the outside piece of silverware and work toward the center.
- When eating soup, the spoon is filled with a movement away from and not toward the body. Food is taken from the side of the spoon into the mouth.
- We cut one bite of meat at a time, then cut another bite. In buttering bread, we break off a portion, butter it, then eat it. We don't butter the whole piece of bread or roll at one time.
- DON'T: lick your fingers... lean on the table with your elbows... use your fingers to push food onto your fork (use knife)... take large portions of food you cannot possibly eat... stir or mash food into a heap on your plate... scrape plates at the table or pile them up... talk with food in your mouth.... chew with your mouth open... reach across the table for food or get up to reach for food... tip back in your chair.
- DO: Send a thank you note to your hostess within a week of his or her hospitality.

Proper table settings (for Americans).

- Generally plates are set about one inch from the edge of the table. Bread and butter plates go to the left of the dinner plate, above the forks. But if salad is served with the main course, the salad plate often replaces the bread and butter plate at the top left.

- Glasses are placed above the knife to the right of the plate.
- Silverware is placed one inch from the table edge.
- The fork is to the left of the plate, with ones to be used first on the outside.
- The knife is to the right of the plate—cutting edge facing in. Butter knives—if used—can be placed across the bread-and-butter or salad plate.
- The spoon is right of the knife, the ones used first on the outside. Never leave a spoon in your cup or glass—after using, put it on your saucer or your plate, not on the table.
- Napkins can be placed in the center of the plate or to the left of forks. A simple fold has the open corners of an oblong fold in the bottom right.
- Allow twenty-four inches for each place setting, thirty inches if there is a side plate for bread or salad.

What to wear. A hostess can wear anything she chooses, provided it is in good taste. Some women love to wear the unusual. Be bold—here is an opportunity to get out your long hostess skirt.

Let your guests know whether the occasion is casual or formal, or a theme party such as wearing costumes or seasonal dress.

In some sections of the country, as in west Texas, I have noticed some men don't remove their cowboy hats even in restaurants. But good manners dictate a man remove his hat in the house, when the flag passes by in a street parade, and so on. What I am saying is, in some locales it is probably not considered bad manners for a man to wear a hat indoors or a woman to wear hair curlers in public, but it still doesn't come across as good manners.

What to avoid. Don't let bitterness eat you up.

One widow complained to me that her children and nieces

and nephews always came to her house to eat but never asked her over. She had to repent and forgive them when she realized she was grateful they felt welcome at her table.

Another woman said, "I told the Lord he could have my house, but it is such a mess I doubt he would want it." She repented and cleaned it up.

Teach your children not to push in line ahead of others in a cafeteria or at church suppers. Gluttony and a "me first" attitude have no place in the Christian walk. You can teach them courtesy. One of my friends says children should be "tamed and trained" by parents investing time with them.

Please, take your crying baby out of a room, church, or from a restaurant table until he or she quiets down. This is simply being considerate of others.

If you have small children, go out with your husband occasionally without them. I know of a five-year-old who had never been without his mom; when they enrolled him for the first time in Sunday school he couldn't manage without her. You can teach them to socialize.

As a guest in another's home. Appreciate what others have. Enjoy the beauty of their things, their uniqueness, without being envious.

Along that same line, don't hesitate to have someone over who has more material possessions than you. One young woman groaned, "I would never have the Martins over, because I don't have fine china dishes, crystal goblets, and sterling silverware like they have." But remember, people want to come to our homes simply for Christian love and fellowship.

ETIQUETTE IN TREATING A GUEST SPEAKER

From my personal experience and from interviewing missionaries, pastors, speakers, and other guests who stay in private homes, this list of suggestions emerged:

- Mail advance details about their speaking engagement—when and where the meeting will be. If they are driving, include a map and explicit directions. Give them a telephone number to leave with their family back home for emergencies while they are with your group.
- Tell them where they will be met at the plane terminal and who to look for (a sign held at the baggage claim is a good idea if they don't know the party meeting them, for instance).
- Be on time when meeting a speaker at a plane or at a prearranged place if they are driving. If they bring a prayer partner, take care of their meals and so forth as well.
- Have someone assigned to them at the meeting to care for their needs—getting them water, showing them where the restroom is, shielding them from a lot of people who would tend to wear them down before the meeting begins. If they want a quiet place to pray, provide it.
- In the room where they are staying overnight (whether a hotel or private home), provide some fresh fruit, juice, and a carafe of water. Some speakers appreciate a snack when they arrive at their room. It is always thoughtful to include a basket with an assortment of traveler's necessities: hand cream, shampoo, shower cap, extra toothbrush, breath mints, aspirin are some of the items I have needed on occasion.
- If the speaker is staying in your home, you may want to give others the pleasure of providing meals as their act of hospitality. Be sensitive. As a guest I have had to wait until ten p.m.—my time—to have dinner with my host's family and, due to the time zone change I was much too tired to enjoy either their company or their food.
- Even if you don't drink coffee, have it available for your guest's breakfast. I once stayed in a beautiful new home

where the hostess ate all her meals out. I had to wait until 10 a.m. at the meeting before I could get anything beyond water. I now take a small jar of instant coffee with me everywhere I go.

PUTTING THESE THINGS INTO PRACTICE

Laura's daughter Kathy, who has a real "musical ear," drove her piano teacher wild with her continual improvising. "Learn to play it by the rules," he admonished her, "the way it is written. Then you can improvise all you want."

Are you ready to improvise? Are these basic ground rules part of your consciousness? Then let's consider some ways we can really enjoy food, fun, and fellowship.

It is important to pray about who to invite. God may impress you to call someone not in your "inner circle" who just might turn out to be the life of the party.

Ask the Lord, too, to give you appropriate ideas for making your guests feel special. You might start by folding table napkins into "fans."

Barbie goes an extra step when her guests include children. For Andrew's third birthday, for instance, she made a gift package for each of the kids.

The tiny tots got colorful bags stuffed with blow-out whistles and five to ten small unbreakable toys. For older kids—so they wouldn't feel left out—Barbie bagged up suitable toys that challenge like rubic's cubes, packages of gummy bears, pencils, and colored marking pens.

Watching them untying the ribbons around their bags, Barbie saw how thrilled the kids were to be part of Andrew's party.

Manners and graciousness know no age, marital status, or gender barriers.

19

Food Fit for a King

Behold, I stand at the door and knock; if anyone hears
My voice and opens the door, I will come in to him, and
will dine with him, and he with Me.

Revelation 3:20 NASB

WHEN IT FIRST DAWNED ON ME that Jesus would like to come
to every meal I prepare—literally as well as spiritually—I
knew I wanted my King to have the best I could cook. Nourishing, tasty, colorful meals, prepared with real thought and
love, served in an atmosphere that shouts "Welcome!" by a vol-
ley of pleasant aromas. We have a special Guest, not just for
Sunday dinner but for Thursday night stew as well.

That is why I pray over every meal I prepare, asking God to
help me make it pleasing to him and to those I serve.

Over the years I discovered no matter what the setting, the
food, or the company, it will always be a banquet when Jesus
dines with us.

"Jesus has no strangers at his table," our pastor said recently. Truly, "Blessed—happy, to be envied—are those who are summoned (invited, called) to the marriage supper of the Lamb..." (Rv 19:9b AMP). Those who have an intimate relationship with the Lord Jesus—the sacrificed Lamb—will one day be invited to the big supper he is going to give. And he, the King of kings, will serve!

YOUR FAMILY MEALTIME

Consider the significance of the mealtime with our family as Dr. Paul Mickey comments:

The dinner table is the traditional symbol and practical center of family togetherness. It is the place where we eat, talk, relax, and enjoy the company of those we love most....

Every mealtime is a time of giving and receiving, serving and being served....

Remember someone has worked to pay for the food. Someone has shopped for the food. Someone has prepared it. Someone has cleaned up the dining area and set the table attractively. As the meal begins, someone will pass a dish to you, and you will pass it on to someone else. Everyone is serving and being served.[1]

What about mealtime other than with our family? Those times when you are being hospitable for Jesus' sake and seem overwhelmed? Now that is when you can (1) do it yourself or (2) enlist help from others, either in your home or by asking those who come to bring a dish.

But whether it is family or company we are going to feed, we can position ourselves first as a Mary at Jesus' feet, then as Martha in serving.

MARTHA'S HOME

Was Martha completely off that day she asked Jesus to tell her sister Mary to get up and help her with the cooking? Remember, Jesus usually had his twelve friends with him when he came to their house.

Robert Morgan, in *Who's Coming to Dinner?* has an interesting insight about that house in Bethany where Jesus felt so "at home." He says:

It is Martha's home, and she is the hostess. The meal takes place around her table.

She, more than likely, was a devoted follower. She took delight in preparing and serving food for Jesus and his companions. Mary's actions annoyed her and she said to Jesus, "Lord, don't you mind that my sister has left me to do everything by myself? Tell her to come and help me!" Jesus did not interpret Mary's behavior as lazy or selfish. He saw her as a seeker of the truth. He saw Martha, unlike Mary, as a more mature disciple. He seemed to be saying, "Martha, my dear, you are worried and bothered about Mary not helping with the meal. The preparation of the meal is important, but Mary doesn't need to be in the kitchen tonight. Be patient. There is not anything more important than what she is doing right now." Jesus supported Mary in her choice to listen at his feet, but at the same time, he demonstrated the highest regard for Martha.[2]

ENLISTING HELP

I have felt like Martha on more than one occasion, desperate for help when I expected a crowd for dinner. As LeRoy and I opened our home for more Bible studies, and thus more meals, my prayer partner Lib offered to be my Martha. "Just let me stay in the background—in the kitchen cooking or washing pots and pans. I don't need to be out with your guests," she said. Many times she rolled up her sleeves, kicked off her shoes and sang to herself in our kitchen while LeRoy and I were out greeting or serving food to several dozen people in our dining room, living room, or on the screened porch.

Lib is the one, remember, who taught me how to "practice hospitality" as we took our meals and our families first to her house and then to mine for months before we were comfortable having others in our own homes.

BIBLICAL INJUNCTION

Even in the Old Testament we see examples of significant happenings around mealtimes. Melchizedek offered bread and wine to Abraham—and Melchizedek was king and priest of God Most High.

Eating a meal together was one way to establish a covenant, even during a time of reconciliation, as with Jacob and Laban (see Gn 31:42, 54).

Jesus himself revered the common meal. At his Last Supper with his disciples as he broke bread and shared the cup, he said, "This do in remembrance of me." He invites us to join the consummation feast, the marriage supper of the Lamb. He really does care about us having joy at mealtime.

Jesus went to a wedding, dined with Pharisees and served dinner-on-the-grounds to more than five thousand people. He even served breakfast to his disciples by the Sea of Galilee after his resurrection.

THE IMPORTANCE OF BREAD

Bethlehem, where Jesus was born, means House of Bread. Pastor Robert Morgan notes that on more than twenty occasions Jesus participated in a meal or told a parable related to a mealtime experience. In many instances, the accounts indicate Jesus shared a meal while he was a guest in someone's house. Jesus himself usually broke bread with his disciples at the end of the day.[3]

According to Morgan, there were at least three reasons bread was of importance to the Jews in Jesus' day:

1. It was the staple of life, the most important food they ate.
2. It was a symbol of God's gift of seed and harvest of grain. One broke bread with respect. Bread was never wasted and even inedible bread was softened with water and fed to birds.
3. Bread was a sacrament of life, a covenant. Even in the Old Testament shared bread signified a covenant.[4]

Morgan also gives us insight into how Jesus' disciples continued to observe the Lord's Supper:

It is no small thing that the "breaking of bread" was the distinctive act of worship of the first believers. It was the continuation of the table covenant that the original disciples had enjoyed with Jesus. Though he was no longer with them in the flesh, they could celebrate together the simple meal at which he had once presided in person. It was a meal that brought back memories of the times when he had broken the bread here on earth. Especially they would recall the Last Supper "on the night he was betrayed." But the spirit in which they partook of the meal was not one of sadness or sorrow. They broke bread "with simple joy" (Acts 2:46). Their eyes were fixed on the banquet of the Kingdom of God. Jesus had promised to drink with them anew at that time.[5]

Jesus said, "I am the bread of life..." (Jn 6:35b). What better way to share him than in breaking bread with friends or strangers in our homes? Or in fellowship around a picnic table or barbecue grill?

EXTRA BLESSINGS AT THE TABLE

Twice a year we had the privilege of breaking bread at the Peter Lord table. How we looked forward to that! We knew as soon as all fifteen to twenty guests were seated around his big table, Pastor Lord would ask, *"What has Jesus done for you this week?"* It was hearing what Jesus had done for each of us *that very week* that excited us and made us anticipate the fellowship.

The table around which Jesus and his disciples gathered in the upper room for his last supper was probably comprised of three tables joined into a U shape, low on the floor, allowing the guests to recline on their left elbow and eat with their right hand. Some disciples may have sat upright on the floor.

I am appalled as I observe how many families never share one meal a day together. Youngsters are off to after-school activities or dad to his civic meetings or mom to her tennis game. When do they communicate the family's values?

Marvin Wilson, in *Our Father Abraham—Jewish Roots of the Christian Faith*, explains why, after the destruction of the Temple, the place where the family dined was like the altar of the Temple:

> The dinner table of the home became, as it were, the altar of the Temple.... Eating was to be more than a physical function; it was to be a spiritual instrument of religious service. Seen as an altar, the table was to be consecrated. It was to be a place where more than food was to be passed; it was also to be set apart, that the words of the Torah might be exchanged....
>
> Around the table, the family sang songs... the father served as priest of his own sanctuary, instructing his family in the words of Torah as one of the priests of old. As the

Israelites came to the Temple to celebrate festivals such as Passover, so the later Jews viewed the home as the center of religious life. It was a place to celebrate holidays and festivals with joy and dedication.[6]

FESTIVALS OF ISRAEL

The New Unger's Bible Dictionary gives insight into the importance of the Jewish feasts and festivals. It tells us that banquets—such as today's circumcision feast when a son is eight days old, or when he has his bar mitzpah at age thirteen—were usually held toward the evening. Some—like a wedding banquet—continued for three to seven days.

Invitations were sent out through the servants some time prior to the banquet. Then another announcement told the expected guests that the arrangements were complete and their presence was looked for (Mt 22:4). "This afternoon summons was sent only to those who had accepted the previous invitation, and to violate that acceptance for trivial reasons could only be viewed as a gross insult."[7]

When guests arrived, a servant received the tablets or cards of the guests who were then taken into the receiving room. After the whole company had arrived, the master of the house shut the door with his own hands, a signal that no others were to be admitted (Lk 13:25; Mt 25:10). The guests were kissed, their feet washed and hair and beard anointed. They were assigned places according to their rank.

Sometimes the guests were furnished a richly embroidered garment to wear during the banquet (Eccl 9:8; Rv 3:4-5). The master of the house presided, and guests were entertained by musicians and dancers.[8]

Festivals of Israel included:
- Feast of Trumpets (Nm 28:11)
- New Moon (Nm 10:10; 28:11-15)

- Feast of Passover and Unleavened Bread (Ex 12:1-28; 23:15; Lv 23:4-8; Nm 28:16-25; Dt 16:16)
- Pentecost, or Feast of Weeks (Ex 34:22; Lv 23:15-16; Nm 28:26; Dt 16:10, 16)
- Day of Atonement (Ex 30:10-30; Lv 16:1-34; Nm 29:7-11)
- Feast of Booths, or Tabernacles (Lv 23:34-43; Nm 29:12-38; Dt 16:13-16; Neh 8:13-18)
- Feast of Purim (Est 9:24-32)
- Feast of Dedication (1 Mc 4:52-59; 2 Mc 10:5-8; Jn 10:22)[9]

GOOD NUTRITION

What is the best, most God-honoring "bread" we can put on our own tables?

I will never forget the day I enrolled in our church's nutrition class. Our teacher Cecil McGee said: "God will hold you responsible for the food you feed your family. You as homemakers are building and molding bodies of your families by what you serve them to eat. Is it nutritious or junk food?"

I was cut to the quick, just remembering last night's luscious key lime pie.

Then he suggested, "For healthy bodies you need three times as many vegetables and fruits as meats, breads, sweets, and fats."

Wow! That class hit me where it hurt most. I wanted to change our food habits to those more geared for good health, but I made a big mistake—I moved too quickly to correct my years of wrong cooking. I went home and immediately removed sugar, sweets, white flour, and soda pop from our pantry and refrigerator. My family was anything but thrilled with my sudden revelations. I should have educated them first, then suggested that together we start cutting back on sweets and soft drinks.

DIETARY LAWS LISTED IN THE BIBLE

The Creator God, desiring that his chosen people maintain good health, gave them detailed laws concerning food consumption which we read about in the Old Testament. He even listed some things to avoid eating, including some scavenger fish and animals. While the New Testament frees people from this law, many of my Christian friends who took that initial nutrition course continue to keep many of the Bible's dietary laws—because they make sense.

Two books gave me lots of needed information from a biblical standpoint: *None of These Diseases* by Dr. S.I. McMillen and *God's Key to Health and Happiness* by Elmer A. Josepheson (both published by Fleming Revell).

NEW TESTAMENT FOODS

We have such a wide variety of foods to choose from in our country, it may be hard to think about the more limited diet the Israelites enjoyed in the time of Jesus. But no doubt they were much healthier.

Evidence indicates that the Israelites ate two regular meals a day: breakfast—a light meal in the morning, and supper—a heavier meal in the evening when the air was cooler.

Bread and fish made up their most usual meal. Bread was sometimes eaten with salt, honey, or broth. Grains and vegetables were also important to their diet.

Bread was made fresh every two or three days. Fruits were sometimes dried and pressed into cakes like apricots, figs, and dates; pomegranates were enjoyed fresh from the trees. Nuts were often roasted: walnuts, pistachios, almonds. Olives, pressed for oil, were most important to a homemaker. There were a variety of vegetables, such as onions, beans, lentils, and cucumbers.

Though fish was the main source of meat, a lamb was roasted at least once a year for Passover. Pork was absolutely forbidden as an unclean animal.[10]

Most of us today eat what we ate at our parents' or grandparents' table. I never tasted Italian, Chinese, or Mexican foods until I married and moved away from home. My mother was a Southern cook who specialized in yeast rolls, cornbread, black-eyed peas, corn on the cob, fried chicken, chicken and dumplings, and tomato and okra stew.

I learned to enjoy many other foods from the numerous friends we made over the years who came from varied backgrounds. Now, when I invite guests for covered dish dinners, I ask them to bring their culinary specialty. I have learned to enjoy many ethnic dishes this way.

An important point: not everyone can open their home for outside guests. Louise, a working wife whose husband will not let her have company, has found ways to be hospitable anyway. She bakes cakes for the pastor's wife and for others hosting missionaries or guest speakers. Once a week she takes a picnic or buys lunch for a co-worker so she can share her Christian faith.

WHERE DO I START?

- Plan meals that are nutritious. Remember, the closer your food is to its natural state, the better it is for you. Nutritionists usually suggest cooking fresh foods first, frozen vegetables as a second choice, and canned ones in a pinch.
- Don't be afraid to experiment with new recipes. Margaret has a practice run on her family a week before her guests are coming, cooking the exact meal she plans. That way she knows how long it is going to take to prepare and she has the recipes "family tested."
- Have two parties back to back—one on Friday, another on

Saturday. You already have your house clean, fresh flowers...

- Serve crunchy fresh raw carrots, celery, cauliflower, or zucchini squash with a vegetable dip made of creamed cottage cheese.
- Instead of carbonated drinks, serve unsweetened fruit juices.
- Sliced banana is a treat when rolled in wheat germ and nut meal. Raisins are good mixed with sunflower seeds and roasted soy nuts. If making a fresh fruit compote, toss white fruit like bananas, pears, or apples in a bit of lemon juice to keep them from discoloring.
- Have a party that suits your personality and mood—sometimes you feel ready for a fish fry (if you caught a freezer full) or a chicken barbecue (when chicken is on sale).

Just be careful not to start like Laura did when Linda and Frank came to supper and the salad dressing wasn't made yet. "Bustling into the kitchen," she told me with a rueful chuckle,

I threw the ingredients into the blender. At the same time I was pushing the chunks of avocado into the blades, I absent-mindedly turned the dial to "start."

The spatula hit the ceiling. Mushy, gooey avocado dressing slithered onto my blouse, my apron, my shoes. Everywhere I looked there were green polka dots—on the floor, the cabinet top, the refrigerator, the painting on the wall, the ceiling—ooh, the ceiling!

I sat down on the floor. My spring was completely unwound. Brooks heard me laughing hysterically and came in to inspect—and help clean up—the mess.

About that time Linda and Frank came in. "I am so glad Frank could see this. He's always telling me I should be neat in the kitchen like you."

My image was ruined. But, so what? After all, in this big

family of God, Frank and Linda are my brother and sister. And a family's love is not based on actions, but on relationships.

Company's coming? There is a short prayer I keep posted on my refrigerator that I copied from Karen Mains' book, *Open Heart, Open Home*:

Oh, Lord, give me love for these varied people. Help me to have an open heart as well as an open door. Let me not be concerned about how things look or how things taste to the exclusion of how people feel. Help me to give them You. Amen.[11]

PART FIVE

Blessings of God's Peace

20

Peace to
This House

My people will live in peaceful dwelling places, in secure homes, in undisturbed places of rest. Isaiah 32:18

S HORTLY AFTER LEROY AND I WERE BAPTIZED in the Holy Spirit, we wanted to let the Lord know, outwardly, that our home was really his. To dedicate it in some way.

I found that *blessing* is defined in the dictionary as "to invoke God's favor upon, to bestow happiness or prosperity, to guard or protect, to consecrate." That was exactly what we wanted: God's blessing.

Jesus told his disciples when they went into a town or village to search for a worthy person and stay at his house. "As you enter the home, give it your greeting. If the home is deserving, let your peace rest on it" (see Mt. 10:12-13a). We wanted our home to be deserving, to have that peace.

When we learned our friend Forrest Mobley, who is an Episcopal priest, was coming through town, we asked him to lead in our house dedication. Kneeling at the coffee table in our living room, we acknowledged God's ownership of our home while Forrest recited a house blessing prayer from his *Manual for Priests:*

Let the almighty power of the Holy God be present in this place to banish from it every unclean spirit, to cleanse it from every residue of evil, and to make it a secure habitation for those who dwell in it; in the name of Jesus Christ our Lord....

We went from room to room as he prayed in each and then asked God's blessing on those who would use or occupy that room. As he was leaving, he added what I later called his *postscript prayer:*

And now, Lord, use this house for your glory and this family *to love others to you.*

I never dreamed that soon after those prayers, I would be sleeping eleven people on pallets on the living room floor while seven others slumbered upstairs. Or that God would send as many as ninety-six people in one week to our house—some to eat, some to fellowship and some to stay overnight.

BIBLICAL EXAMPLES

Dedication ceremonies with appropriate speeches were common in Israel's history. For instance, Psalm 30 is a song sung at the dedication of the house of David. In Deuteronomy 20:5, the question is asked, "Has anyone built a new house and not dedicated it?" as though this was an expected action. Of course the dedication of the house of God was celebrated with joy— read about it in Ezra 6:16.

In Judaism, one of the most important family values is a peaceful home—*shalom bayit.* Jesus taught, "Blessed are the peacemakers," and Paul identified peace as a fruit of the Spirit. A Christian home, then, should be a peaceful home. *Shalom bayit.*

HOME A REFUGE

Tom White says it well:

The Christian receives the very life of God and becomes a "temple of the Holy Spirit" (1 Cor 6:19) so that he can "live with them and walk among them" (2 Cor 6:16). Therefore, those places where we live and work should be dedicated as God's holy domain, endowed with the power of his presence and used for His redemptive purposes.[1]

White believes there are positive things we can do to insure a more peace-filled home:

- Remove desecration. Evil spirits can pollute places with their unholy presence. Such demonization usually occurs when mortal beings commit immoral acts that open the door to the activity of demons.... Even when the perpetrators have left the scene, evil spirits may linger, hoping to prey upon unsuspecting newcomers.
- Consecrate and dedicate the place to God.... Verbal, visible pronouncement is important in declaring this intention.
- Honor the Lord. Fill your home with objects and activities that bring glory to God.
- Maintain protection. Pray unceasingly with alertness.... Exercise spiritual authority.... Discern and deal with evil

influences. Be cautious about inviting strangers into your home.... Confront ungodly values.... Resolve family tensions.

• Establish a godly heritage. The refuge you are establishing has exciting ramifications for your children and *their* children (see Ps 103:17-18).[2]

MODERN EXAMPLES

Laura and Brooks' home group met to pray at the house of Gene and Jane, while they were remodeling it. They had previously rented the house to people who were into drugs and the occult. There was a residue of satanic oppression permeating the whole downstairs—so strong it was uncomfortable to even walk through the rooms. So Gene had asked the group to come over before they moved in.

"One of the men led our prayer," Laura remembers. "Then as soon as someone said, 'Let's hold hands,' we all knew that was the way God was leading. And the very instant we did, three things happened."

I had the strong impression of a force pushing out from our circle through the whole house.... One of the men "saw" Daniel in the lions' den—unhurt, the lions' mouths shut.

It was when we came in one accord and touched hands that we felt power stronger than any electrical force—power in the name of Jesus Christ.

The word that came to one of us during the prayer was "sweep and garnish." Sweep up the remodeling debris and get rid of anything the spiritist people had left behind. Then the word was to fill the house with good—God's—people and good things, like fresh paint, carpeting, and Jane's figurine of a dove.

Today when we walk into that house, we can feel the peace. Never again have they experienced the oppression.

Jan, recently widowed, moved back to her hometown and bought a house. She invited some friends to bless it and asked Don, an elder in her church, to lead the dedication.

Don prayed that this house would be God's provision for Jan and her son while they laid the foundations for their heavenly mansion. He prayed for the Lord's continuing provision for Jan in everything she needed.

He read from Deuteronomy 6, where God told the people to write his word on the door frames of their houses and on their gates. Then Don directed the friends to go into each room and anoint the doorposts and the gates—which in this case were the pillars of the front porch—as they prayed for the people and activities housed there:

- In the living room—that company would know God dwelt there in his people.
- In the bedrooms—that God would give his beloved sweet sleep and would station angels to watch over them as they slept.
- In the kitchen—that God would sanctify the food prepared there, eaten with thanks to him for their daily bread....

This done, the twenty or so friends and family gathered in a circle, held hands, and sang "Blest Be the Tie That Binds."

God's peace reigns in Jan's life and in her house.

If you have never had the absolute delight of showing someone to a spotless and fragrant room with fresh sheets and a little welcome note on the pillow, and then sitting them down at your table where your love for them has provoked you to make a meal that will bless their body, soul, and spirit, then can I invite you to indulge in the pleasure of the company of the one whom you serve and to celebrate being together? Invite Jesus into your midst, and you will have stepped into a dimension you won't want to leave.[3]

During the five-year span while Brooks and Laura were building their dream house, they lived in four different condominiums. Each time they moved, their home group came to bless that dwelling, even though they knew it would be only temporary. Jamie would invariably wander into Laura's home office and pray for God's anointing on her as she would write.

"What a joy, to have that sense of unity in our working together, knowing God's hand was blessing," Laura said.

LeRoy and I have moved into several dwellings since Forrest Mobley blessed our home many years ago. But in each one we have had a dedication ceremony. Once, on our twentieth-fifth wedding anniversary, we had a house dedication with some seventy-five people dropping by for open house.

We did not always have a pastor to dedicate our house or apartment, so we did the ceremony ourselves with a few close friends. You may want to have a house blessing, too. Make it a special occasion, even if you do not have the pastor there and even if it is not new, but only because you have never actually dedicated it to the Lord. One thing I can guarantee: you will be blessed, all who enter will be blessed, and God will be glorified.

Yours will be a house of many blessings.

The Lord bless you and keep you; the Lord make his face shine upon you and be gracious to you; the Lord turn his face toward you and give you peace. Numbers 6:24-26

Epilogue

AFTER I FINISHED my part of this book, I found myself in an Indian village high in the Guatemalan mountains. Sixteen of us were on our first United States Aglow overseas outreach mission.

After distributing medicines, clothes, gospel messages, and love to the people who had come to the rustic church, we began hiking even higher up the mountain. Through cornfields, past coffee trees, higher still higher until we could almost touch the clouds as they rolled in about us.

Our purpose for this highest climb was to pronounce a blessing on the house of a church deacon and leave some clothes for his children. The modest one-room wooden shanty had a simple tin roof, and a dirt floor where baby chicks scratched at our feet. My eye was drawn to a rusty can holding some delicate white wild flowers—a woman's touch of beauty to turn her modest house into a home. Truly we felt the presence of the Lord, as we praised God with songs in three different languages.

Edging my way down the mountain, I thought of the elegant three-story brick home of a relative I had visited a few months earlier. The husband had fussed when he discovered a few drops of water from the swimming pool on his kitchen's hardwood floors. "Do you care more about people or things?" I asked him, feeling uncomfortable because of his constant mention of the cost and grandeur of his house. He just shrugged his shoulders.

Where did I feel more at home?

I felt more at home in the Indian woman's hut where a

kerosene lantern or her cook stove lit with little sticks provided the only source of light. Jesus, the Light of the world was reflected there.

As I continued my precarious walk down the mountain toward the truck that would take us still another two hours downward, I thought about a thirteen-year-old delinquent girl who spoke to our congregation one Sunday night just before she was released by the state to return to her own parents.

"Many of you people in this church helped me while I was in the girl's school in your town. On weekends you had me in your homes, you fed me, even gave me clothes. But best of all, you introduced me to Jesus. I am so glad of what he has done for me, I want to thank him...." she said.

Then her eyes lit up, "But you are him here so I will thank you."

You are him here! Her words penetrated into our hearts. Pastor Lord had wooden plaques made for members to display in their home: "YOU ARE HIM HERE" they proclaimed. A reminder that while here on earth, we are his feet, his heart, his extended hands. We, his followers, are indeed him here. And I know Jesus puts people before things.

Oh Lord, help me not to forget this, I pray.

Quin Sherrer
Dallas, Texas

Notes

ONE
Welcome to Our Home

1. Anne Ortlund, *Disciplines of the Home* (Dallas: Word, 1990), 41.

THREE
Decorating on a Tight Budget

1. Vivian Hall, *Be My Guest,* from the foreword by Helga Henry (Chicago: Moody Press, 1979).
2. Hall, 9.
3. Georg Andersen, *Interior Decorating: a Reflection of the Creator's Design* (Minneapolis: Bethany House, 1983), 34.
4. Gerald M. Knox, ed., *All About Your House: Decorating Your Home* (Des Moines: Meredith, 1985), 40.
5. Mary C. Crowley, *Decorate Your Home With Love* (Old Tappan, NJ: Revell, 1986), 7.

FIVE
Family First

1. Edith Schaeffer, *What Is a Family?* (Old Tappan, NJ: Revell, 1975), 167-168.
2. Dennis and Ruth Gibson, *The Sandwich Years* (Grand Rapids: Baker, 1991), 9-10.
3. "The Christian Family Standard" adopted by the Family Life Committee of the Lutheran Church, Missouri Synod. Quoted in Helping Families Through the Church (St. Louis: Concordia, 1957).

SIX
Extended Family

1. J.I. Packer, Merrill C. Tenney, and William White, Jr., *The Bible Almanac* (Nashville: Thomas Nelson, Guideposts edition, 1980), 416.
2. Packer, 417.
3. Marvin R. Wilson, *Our Father Abraham—Jewish Roots of the Christian Faith* (Grand Rapids: Eerdmans, 1989), 214-215.
4. Wilson, 216.

SEVEN
Hospitality and Tiny Tots

1. Richard Dobbins, Ph.D., "Bringing Them Up with Loving Discipline," *Logos Journal*, (Sept/Oct 1977): 24.
2. Ibid.
3. Linda Davis Zumbehl, *Homebodies* (Springfield, PA: Whitaker House, 1991), 20.

EIGHT
Tradition Keepers

1. Vivian Hall, *Be My Guest* (Chicago: Moody, 1979), 98.

NINE
Open House Blessings

1. Last 7 pages adapted from "The Blessings of Open-House Hospitality," by Quin Sherrer, *Charisma* (January 1979): 67-70.

TEN
The Prophet's Chamber

1. James M. Freeman, *Manners and Customs of the Bible* (Plainfield, NJ: Logos, 1972), 171-172.

ELEVEN
The Innkeepers

1. *Encyclopedia Judaic*, Vol. 8 (Jerusalem: Keter Publishing House, 1972), 1030-1032.
2. Francis A. Schaeffer, *The Church at the End of the 20th Century* (Downers Grove, IL: InterVarsity, 1976), 108.
3. Schaeffer, 111.

TWELVE
Angels or Strangers?

1. Vivian Hall, *Be My Guest* (Chicago: Moody, 1979), 34-35.
2. Jack W. Hayford, ed. *The Spirit Filled Life Bible* (Nashville: Thomas Nelson, 1991), 1940, 1942.

THIRTEEN
Singular Hospitality

1. Carolyn A. Koons and Michael J. Anthony, *Single Adult Passages* (Grand Rapids: Baker, 1991), 206.
2. Koons and Anthony, 211.
3. James Dobson, ed., *Focus on the Family* magazine (February 1992): 16.

FOURTEEN

Who Will "Titus" Me?

1. Ted Engstrom, *The Fine Art of Mentoring* (Brentwood, TN: Wolgemuth & Hyatt, 1989), 144.

2. Lucibel Van Atta, *Women Encouraging Women* (Portland, OR: Multnomah, 1987), 78.

FIFTEEN

The Proverbs 31 Principle

1. Linda Davis Zumbehl, *Homebodies* (Springfield, PA: Whitaker House, 1991), 20.

2. Matthew Henry's *Commentary of the Whole Bible* (McLean, VA: McDonald Publishing Co., originally written in 1710), 976.

3. Adapted from memo, "Preparation for the Future," by elders of Park Avenue Baptist Church (Titusville, Florida).

4. For a complete list of items, see *Project Readiness* by Louise E. Nelson, a guide to family emergency preparedness, Horizon Publishers, P.O. Box 490, Bountiful, UT 84010.

5. For more information, write to Denise Boggs, Keepers at Home Creations, 4460 Westview Lane, Titusville, FL 32780.

6. Baukje Doornenbal, *Homemaking* (Colorado Springs: NavPress, 1981), 4.

SIXTEEN

Reciprocal Living

1. Karl A. Barden, *The Activated Church* (Shippensburg, PA: Destiny Image, 1992), 92-93.

2. Henri Daniel-Rops, *Daily Life in the Time of Jesus* (Ann Arbor: Servant, 1980), 309.

3. Jamie Buckingham, "The Message of Suffering," *Corridors Leading to Hope* newsletter, Vol. 2, No. 12, (June 2, 1983).

SEVENTEEN

Commitment to Community

1. C.W. Brister, *Pastoral Care in the Church* (San Francisco: Harper San Francisco, 1992), 149.

2. Leith Anderson, *A Church for the 21st Century* (Minneapolis: Bethany House, 1992), 35.

3. Zevi Scharfstein, comp. *The New Comprehensive Shilo English-Hebrew Dictionary* (New York, NY: Shilo Publishing House, 1973), 295.

4. Kenneth A. Schmidt, *Finding Your Way Home* (Ventura, CA: Regal Books, 1990), 264.

5. Rick Joyner, "The Revolution is at Hand," Pineville, NC, *The Morning Star Journal*, Vol. 2, No. 1 (1992), 58.
6. Carl F. George, *Prepare Your Church for the Future* (Tarrytown: Revell, 1991), 120.

EIGHTEEN
Manners and Graciousness

1. *Encyclopedia Judaic*, Vol. 8 (Jerusalem: Keter Publishing House, 1972), 1031.

NINETEEN
Food Fit for a King

1. Paul A. Mickey with William Proctor, *Charisma* magazine (March 1986): 75, reprint from their book *Tough Marriage* (William Morrow & Co., 1986).
2. Robert C. Morgan, *Who's Coming to Dinner?* (Nashville: Abingdon, 1992), 57.
3. Morgan, 17.
4. Morgan, 18-19.
5. Morgan, 134.
6. Marvin R. Wilson, *Our Father Abraham* (Grand Rapids: Eerdmans, 1989), 215.
7. Merrill F. Unger, *The New Unger's Bible Dictionary*, R.K. Harrison, ed., (Chicago: Moody, 1988), 141.
8. Unger, 142.
9. Unger, 407.
10. Henri Daniel-Rops, *Daily Life in the Time of Jesus* (Ann Arbor: Servant, 1961), 197-204.
11. Karen Burton Mains, *Open Heart, Open Home* (Elgin: David C. Cook, 1976), 51.

TWENTY
Peace to This House

1. Thomas B. White, *The Believer's Guide to Spiritual Warfare* (Ann Arbor: Servant, 1990), 104.
2. White, adapted from 105-110.
3. Dale Garratt, *The Pleasure of Your Company* (Eastbourne, England: Kingsway Publications, 1983), 11.

Recommended Books

- *How to Live on Almost Nothing and Have Plenty* (a practical introduction to small-scale sufficient living), by Janet Chadwick (New York: Alfred A. Knopf, 1979).
- *Back to Basics* (how to learn and enjoy traditional American skills) (Pleasantville, NY: The Reader's Digest Association, 1981).
- *Homebodies* (the homemaker's guide to organization and contentment), by Linda Davis Zumbehl (Springdale, PA: Whitaker House 1991).
- *Prepare Your Church for the Future* (introducing the meta-church: large enough to celebrate, small enough to care), by Carl F. George (Tarrytown, NY: Fleming Revell, 1991).
- *Our Father Abraham—Jewish Roots of the Christian Faith*, by Marvin R. Wilson (Grand Rapids: Eerdmans, 1989).
- *The Messianic Passover Haggadah* (bringing celebrations of the Bible into your home), by Barry and Steffi Rubin, 6204 Park Heights Avenue, Baltimore, MD 21215; phone: 410/358-6471 (Baltimore: Lederer Foundation, 1989).
- *Daily Life in the Time of Jesus*, by Henri Daniel-Rops (Ann Arbor: Servant, 1981).
- *Disciplines of the Home*, by Anne Ortlund (Dallas: Word, 1990).
- *Interior Decorating—a Reflection of the Creator's Design*, by Georg Andersen (Minneapolis: Bethany House, 1983).
- *Decorate Your Home with Love*, by Mary C. Crowley (Old Tappan, NJ: Fleming Revell, 1986).
- *Open Heart, Open Home* (how to find joy through sharing your home with others), by Karen Burton Mains (Elgin: David C. Cook, 1976).
- *Things Happen When Women Care* (hospitality and friendship in today's busy world), by Emilie Barnes (Eugene, OR: Harvest House, 1990).
- *Hidden Art*, by Edith Schaeffer (Wheaton: Tyndale, 1975).
- *Who Cares?* (cultivating the fine art of loving one another), by Gayle G. Roper (Wheaton: Harold Shaw Publishers, 1992).

- *Women Mentoring Women*, by Vicki Kraft (Chicago: Moody, 1992).
- *When Mothers Must Work* (How to make working work for you and your family), by Carolyn Sedgwick (Springdale, PA: Whitaker, 1988).
- *The Teenage Book of Manners... Please*, by Fred Hartley and Family (Westwood, NJ: Barbour Books, 1991).
- *None of These Diseases* (sacred writings predate modern medicine), by S.I. McMillen, M.D. (Old Tappan, NJ: Fleming Revell/Spire Books, 1973).

OTHER BOOKS BY QUIN AND LAURA

- *How to Pray for Your Children* (from unborn to adulthood; praying for both godly and wayward children), by Quin Sherrer (Lynnwood, WA: Aglow Publications, 1986).
- *How to Forgive Your Children* (how to forgive yourself, God, your parents, and your children—the prodigal and the godly), by Quin Sherrer with Ruthanne Garlock (Lynnwood, WA: Aglow Publications, 1989).
- *How to Pray for Your Family and Friends* (releasing God's power in the lives of your spouse, parents, brothers, sisters, neighbors—even your enemies), by Quin Sherrer with Ruthanne Garlock (Ann Arbor: Servant, 1990).
- *The Spiritual Warrior's Prayer Guide* (how to safeguard your family and spiritual leaders in prayer), by Quin Sherrer and Ruthanne Garlock (Ann Arbor: Servant, 1992).
- *A Woman's Guide to Spiritual Warfare* (a how-to manual for prayer and spiritual warfare on topics that women face), by Quin Sherrer and Ruthanne Garlock (Ann Arbor: Servant, 1991).
- *Making Your Husband Feel Loved* (nineteen prominent women share secrets of happy marriages), compiled by Betty Malz with Laura Watson (Lake Mary, FL: Creation House, 1990).
- *Collision Course* (the biography of a well-known evangelist who was divorced and remarried—and God put him back in the pulpit), by Del Storey with Laura Watson (Plainfield, NJ: Logos International, 1977).

About the Authors

QUIN SHERRER, author of several books on prayer, has traveled in eight countries recently speaking on her book topics. She holds a B.S. degree in journalism from Florida State University and has a background in secular and religious writing, having published for numerous Christian publications. She is a winner of *Guidepost Magazine* Writer's contest and the 1990 Writer of the Year for the Florida Writer's In Touch Christian Conference. She serves on the International Board of Women's Aglow Fellowship.

Laura Watson, personal assistant to the late author Jamie Buckingham, helped in editing most of his forty-five books. Laura was the long time editor of The Trumpet newsletter published by The Tabernacle in Melbourne, Florida pastored by Jamie Buckingham. She also served as book editor for *Ministries Today* Magazine published by Strang Communications.

Laura and Quin have been prayer partners for two decades. This is their first co-authorship.